Strategies for
Whitetails

Text and photography by

Charles J. Alsheimer

www.CharlesAlsheimer.com

©2006 Charles J. Alsheimer
Published by

kp **krause publications**
A subsidiary of F+W Media, Inc.

700 East State Street • Iola, WI 54990-0001
715-445-2214 • 888-457-2873
www.krausebooks.com

Our toll-free number to place an order or obtain
a free catalog is (800) 258-0929.

Library of Congress Control Number: 2005906851

ISBN 13-digit: 978-0-89689-331-3
ISBN 10-digit: 0-89689-331-6

Designed by Sharon Laufenberg
Edited by Dan Shideler

Printed in China

Dedication

To

Jack Brauer

Al Hofacker

Pat Durkin

Dan Schmidt

Debbie Knauer

Hugh McAloon

Contents

Dedication 3
Foreword 6
Acknowledgments 7
About The Author 8
Introduction 8

SECTION I: The Animal 9

Chapter 1: Nature's Superstar 10
Chapter 2: Lover's And Fighters 18
Chapter 3: Anatomy Of the Rut 28
Chapter 4: When the Rut Goes Bonkers 38

SECTION II: The Hunt 47

Chapter 5: Deer Activity: Triggers & Suppressors 48
Chapter 6: Structure Your Hunt 58
Chapter 7: Hunting the Pre-Rut 68
Chapter 8: Timing the Rut 78
Chapter 9: Hunting the Rut 88
Chapter 10: Hunting the Post-Rut 98
Chapter 11: What Is Realistic 108
Chapter 12: Bagging the Memories 118

SECTION III: Better Deer: Better Hunting 127

Chapter 13: Quality Deer Management 128
Chapter 14: Build It and They Will Come 138
Chapter 15: Better Food Plots for Better Deer 148

SECTION IV: What Matters Most 159

Chapter 16: My Journey 160
Chapter 17: More Than An Animal to Me 170
Chapter 18: What Matters Most 180

Index 191

Foreword

As we climbed the steep grade at an altitude approaching 10,000 feet, my friend Charlie Alsheimer paused to check on the little guy following in his footsteps. He chidingly remarked, "I thought you were in shape, Bernier. What do I have to do, carry you up the mountain?"

Standing there, nearly on top of the world in the Alberta Rockies, I was gasping for breath and wondering at the same time, "How can a guy twelve years my senior be making this ascent with what seems like little effort?"

Ultimately, the intense climb led to the experience of a lifetime photographing bighorn rams on top of the world. We returned to the bottom of the mountain later in the day incredibly grateful for the opportunity God had given us. Shooting alongside Charlie had been a great chance for me to learn about the craft of nature photography. Little did I realize he would show me something far more important on the trip back to town.

As we rounded a bend in the road, a traffic jam came into view. Vacated cars were lined up on both sides of the highway. At least fifty photographers with long lenses were congregated in an open meadow along the side of the road. Charlie pulled the car to a stop, jumped out, grabbed his camera and tripod and exclaimed, "Let's see what this is all about!"

Feeling tired, I reluctantly followed him at a distance. The "boys of autumn" were out in force, photographing a big bull elk that was making every attempt to breed a cow. And now, even after the physically demanding climb we had just completed, Charlie was out there in the thick of it, competing for position with men half his age.

I didn't take any photos as I sat there watching. Instead, I smiled inwardly and marveled at my friend as he scurried about to get ready for the next series of shots. With his cap turned backward and a grin on his face, he tenaciously pursued the elk as if he had never experienced anything like this before.

What makes Charlie Alsheimer so good at what he does? What sets him apart from others? He is blessed with considerable ability, but I believe the root of his success lies in what he demonstrated in that Alberta meadow. His undying pursuit of excellence results in a willingness to stay out there when everyone else has called it a day. He possesses the dogged determination and hopeful outlook you need to get that final "stunner" of a photo. You won't find this trait being taught in any institution of higher learning; it's a quality that comes from deep within.

It's easy to look at a guy like Charlie and attribute his accomplishments to sheer luck. But let me assure you, that is not the case. I know this man and I know what drives him. The heights he has reached are the result of hard work, fierce determination, uncompromising integrity, and God's gracious hand of blessing. Charlie's focus and resolve have led him to spend countless hours huddled behind the lens of his camera. In the process, he has learned more about white-tailed deer behavior than anyone I have ever met, and trust me, I've met some of the best in the business.

There are many gifted nature photographers, a lot of big-name celebrities that kill trophy whitetails with uncanny regularity, and a considerable number of knowledgeable deer behaviorists. Rarely, however, will you find someone who is all three of these rolled into one. Charlie is one of the few. He is truly the complete package.

As you begin reading *Strategies for Whitetails*, remember one thing: the strategies discussed in this book were developed and fine-tuned by a man who has spent a lifetime observing and documenting virtually every aspect of whitetail behavior. That man just happens to be Charles J. Alsheimer, which means you're in for an incredible learning experience.

R.G. Bernier
Northeast Field Editor
Deer and Deer Hunting magazine
August 7, 2005

Acknowledgments

In September of 1979 I embarked on a journey that most said was impossible. I left the corporate world of sales and marketing to chase a dream of becoming an outdoor writer and nature photographer. Admittedly it was a "crap shoot – a pipe dream," but dreams do come true, so I set out to chase that dream. On my office wall I have a wooden sign that contains this quote: "Live Your Dreams." Well, for the last 25+ years I've lived the dream.

For starters, I've been blessed to have lived in America – one of the few places on Earth where you can chase your dreams and actually catch them. Secondly, America is made up of some incredible people. What I've been able to accomplish required some degree of talent but the bulk of the credit for whatever successes that have come my way go to those who made it all possible. I've been blessed by being in the presence of some very special, caring people.

Whenever you try to acknowledge those who have helped you along the way you run the risk of leaving someone out. Hopefully I will not do that here but if I do, please forgive me.

Charles H. and Eleanor Alsheimer: Though you are both gone I want to thank you for introducing me to the wonders of nature. Dad, you sacrificed a lot by taking me with you on your hunts. And mom, thank you for encouraging me to be all I could be.

Carla: To the love of my life, I say thanks. You've made it possible for me to fly – you gave me my wings, kept me on course, and encouraged me all along the way. Thank you for being a wonderful wife for over 34 years and my best friend.

Aaron: Aside from being an incredible photo model you're the greatest son any man could hope to have. For the past 27 years we've had a storybook relationship as a father and son. Together we've climbed to the top of the Rockies, bushwhacked our way through the Alaskan tundra, canoed the Everglades to the Atlantic Ocean, explored many of the wild haunts in North America and spent untold hours in the whitetail forest. It's been a special trip. Thanks for loving me, thanks for being there, and thanks for the memories.

Paul Daniels: Thanks to one of my best friends in the world. You've always been willing to do anything I've needed – from modeling to caring for the deer operation. I love ya, man!

Terry Rice: Thanks for all the early-morning modeling sessions. You're great at what you do and your friendship means a lot to me.

Jack Brauer and Al Hofacker: You launched *Deer and Deer Hunting* magazine, a magazine no one thought possible.

Then you took a chance on an obscure farm guy from western New York State who had a big dream. You two gave me my first real break in this business and coached and nurtured me through the early years. It is doubtful I'd be where I am today without you. Thanks for who you are; thanks for what you did for me.

Pat Durkin and Dan Schmidt: Of all the editors I've worked with in the outdoor world over the last 25+ years you're the best. During your time in the *Deer and Deer Hunting* editor's chair you gave me a lot of encouragement and leeway – you helped me grow. I'm forever indebted for all you've both done for me. I count our friendship very special.

Debbie Knauer and Hugh McAloon: As *Deer and Deer Hunting* publishers you reached out to make me a part of the *DDH* team. The relationship I forged with each of you has been special. Thanks for all you have done to mold me into what I am.

Haas Hargrave and Dick Snavely: These two outstanding businessmen and outdoorsman encouraged me to pursue a career in the outdoor field when others said it was financially impossible. Their counsel helped birth a dream that became a reality.

Craig Dougherty: We're not only country neighbors but we also share the vision for better deer and better deer hunting. Thanks for all your insight and advice over the years. You are a great friend.

Dick Bernier: Thank you for your research help and "big woods" tracking insight. But most of all thank you for your friendship. You are the best deer tracker in the business. Stay on the track!

Bob and Alma Avery: Thank you for loving me, feeding me, "adopting" me into your family, and allowing me to photograph on your estate. Your mountain spread is truly heaven on earth.

Jim, Charlie, Jack, Aaron, Paul, Whitey, Spook, Dodger, Bambi, Bucky, Carla, Susie and Buttercup: Without you, I wouldn't have learned what I know about whitetails. Collectively you have taught me more than all the wildlife biologists or scientific journals combined. Thanks for allowing me a window into the whitetail's hidden world.

Last, but most importantly, I want to thank Jesus Christ for the gift of life. To some, the mere mention of His name is a turn-off. To others, He is looked at as a crutch. But to me, He is the reason for living, the reason for hope, the reason for the successes I've had. I owe what I have today to the Grace of God. It's that simple. I serve a great and loving God and without Him none of this would be possible.

About the Author

Charles Alsheimer is an award-winning outdoor writer, nature photographer, lecturer, and whitetail consultant from Bath, New York. Alsheimer was born and raised on a farm and has devoted his life to photographing, writing and lecturing about the wonders of God's creation. His specialty – both as a writer and photographer – is the white-tailed deer.

He is the northern field editor for *Deer and Deer Hunting* magazine and host of their national television show, *Deer & Deer Hunting TV*, which airs on the Outdoor Channel. He is also a contributing editor for *Whitetail News*.

In the past 25 years, Alsheimer's work has taken him across North America. His photography has won numerous state and national contests, and his articles and photographs have appeared in nearly every major outdoor publication, including *Outdoor Life, Field & Stream, Sports Afield*, Harris Publications and *Deer and Deer Hunting*. In addition, he has written five popular books on the whitetail and co-authored a sixth. Alsheimer also owns and operates a white-tailed deer research facility and provides consulting services to various segments of the whitetail industry.

In a national poll conducted in January 2000 by *Deer and Deer Hunting*, Alsheimer was honored as one of deer hunting's top five inspirational leaders of the past century. The ballot included the names of nearly 60 scientists, manufacturers, politicians, celebrities, communicators, and hunters. These individuals were selected for their efforts to enhance America's understanding of the white-tailed deer and promote the sport of deer hunting through such means as establishing national forests, developing camouflage patterns, and writing popular books. When the results of the survey were compiled, Alsheimer ranked third behind bowhunter Fred Bear and conservationist Aldo Leopold. President Theodore Roosevelt and outdoor apparel designer Bill Jordan finished fourth and fifth, respectively. This honor illustrates the respect America's deer hunters hold for Alsheimer.

Alsheimer lives with his wife on their farm in rural upstate New York. Additional information about him and his work can be found on his website, www.CharlesAlsheimer.com.

Introduction

They say that if you live long enough you'll see about everything. Well, I may not have seen everything there is to know about whitetail hunting, but I've witnessed much over the last 40 years. The journey has been amazing.

When I began carrying a gun to the deer woods in 1964, whitetail hunting was much different from today. Back then only the most serious deer hunters in our area of western New York State had sights on their shotguns – most simply had their favorite bird gun double as their deer slayer. Nor did anyone I knew wear special deer hunting clothing back then – their farm clothes were what they wore to hunt deer. The more they reeked of farm smells the better they thought they were.

Deer hunting strategies such as hunting rub lines, scrape lines or using deer calls were unheard of. Yes, the deer hunting world I grew up in was night and day removed from today—except for one thing. The animal.

Today's whitetail is the same as the whitetail of the last 100 years. It's still just as elusive, just as challenging, and perhaps a bit smarter. The only thing that has changed when it comes to deer hunting is the bells and whistles we use to help outsmart them.

Last fall I began hunting whitetails in mid-October and didn't stop until the eve of Christmas. Consequently, I had a lot of time to think. Much of what I thought about was what the whitetail has brought to my life. I hate to think what my life would have been like without the white-tailed deer. This animal not only introduced me to nature but provided me with a profession. My childhood fire was lit by the graceful figure of a mature buck running across a plowed field on our farm. That fire has kept me heading back to the woods for nearly 45 years.

Over the years I've gone through a process of sorts in my relationship with the whitetail. When I was a young boy, all I ever wanted to do was be able to see deer. Then, during my teen-age years, the thrill of hunting whitetails was a big part of my life. As I progressed from being a young man to middle-aged my view of the whitetail became more complex. By the time I reached 40 the thrill of the hunt took on a new dimension as the desire to know all I could about whitetails became the centerpiece of my hunting experience.

Even though I've passed the half century point in my life I still love to hunt whitetails. But the challenge of the hunt has been surpassed by the desire to understand all aspects of the whitetail, from their behavior to how to better manage them.

In your hands you hold a book that took about four months to birth, from writing to selecting the photos. However, I can assure you that what is sandwiched between these covers has been fifty years in the making. This is a story about my journey with the white-tailed deer: how I hunt them, photograph them, manage them and love them. What you are about to read and view has been gleaned from my experiences in the woods, both as a hunter and photographer. My whitetail journey was birthed on a northeastern potato farm. Along the way I spread my wings to pursue whitetails from Nova Scotia to Florida to Texas to Idaho to Saskatchewan and points in between. It's been an incredible journey.

During my lifetime I've spent hundreds of hours huddled behind a camera and sitting in deer stands. From these experiences I've come to realize how much we've learned about this great animal. At the same time I'm struck by how little we know. In the text that follows I hope to shed some light on the many mysteries of the white-tailed deer.

You are about to enter the world of what I consider to be the greatest game animal roaming North America. Enjoy your journey.

Charles Alsheimer
October 29, 2005

The Animal

CHAPTERS ONE • TWO • THREE • FOUR

CHAPTER 1

Nature's Superstar

I've had a storied career as a nature photographer and outdoor writer. My travels with camera have taken me from Australia's outback to the wilds of Alaska and points in between. During this journey I've filmed a vast array of wildlife, from kangaroos to grizzlies.

When it comes to wild animals there is friendly debate as to which animal ranks as North America's most athletic. Some argue that squirrels, big cats or mountain sheep are the best all-around when it comes to athleticism. Others say antelope, bears, or birds of prey top the list.

There is no question that some animals can run faster, jump farther and see better than white-tailed deer. However, after pursuing most of North America's big game animals with camera I've yet to find one that can offer the whole physical package like white-tailed deer. Few animals can live with man and beast and still survive. The whitetail can. In short it can outmaneuver, outjump, outrun and outsurvive anything walking the continent –including man.

When whitetails want to they can run up to 40 miles per hour.

Few animals are as graceful as a whitetail. They are the ultimate gymnast.

▶ Speed Demon

You don't have to spend much time around whitetails to know they have speed to burn. There may be a few animals in North America that can outrun a whitetail, but when it comes to putting the pedal to the metal or turning on a dime, the whitetail has few peers.

On more than one occasion I've been able to monitor a deer running in the open alongside an automobile. The top speed I've witnessed was slightly over 40 miles per hour. This is pretty impressive considering the world's fastest human barely tops 20 mph. Of course a whitetail really shines in an obstacle-strewn forest, where deadfalls, thick brush and other natural hazards are the norm. Certainly topography and natural conditions dictate a deer's speed in each situation, but it's safe to say that a mature whitetail can easily run 25 mph in a forest setting.

The consensus among experts is that whitetails are more sprinters than marathon runners. I'd have to agree with this assessment though I have seen whitetails run up to a mile before stopping.

▶ Scale Tall Buildings?

Over the years I've heard all kinds of statements concerning how high a whitetail can jump. Some say a deer can clear a seven-foot-high fence from a standing position. Others say it can easily clear an eight- to 10-foot high fence if it has a running start.

During the last 25 years of observing and raising whitetails up close and personal I have to admit that I've never seen one clear an eight-foot high fence. I have seen many that have tried, but none made it. My guess is that the right deer under the right conditions may be able to clear an eight-foot fence, but I've never seen it done. In every case where I've seen a buck or doe try to leap a high fence they've hit it between 6-1/2 and 7-1/2 feet high.

Whether they can clear eight-, nine- or 10-foot-high fences is immaterial. What impresses me most about the whitetail's jumping ability is that it stands only 36 to 42 inches high at the shoulders but is capable of catapulting its body over obstacles more than twice its height. That's impressive! By comparison, Olympic high jumpers cannot clear an eight-foot-high bar and most are well over six feet tall.

In my mind a whitetail's horizontal jumping prowess surpasses its ability to clear high fences. A deer's ability to chew up yards of ground with each bound is legendary. During the rut two years ago I

When conditions are right a whitetail can easily clear a seven-foot-high fence.

photographed an incredible breeding-party sequence (see Chapter 4). An estrous doe was being pursued by a dominant buck and several lesser-racked bucks. In one exchange the dominant buck chased an intruding subordinate buck. With the dominant buck bearing down on him the subordinate buck turned on a dime and ran for his life. Unfortunately a four-foot-high cattle fence stood in his way.

At full throttle the subordinate buck cleared the fence in one fluid motion. As impressive as this was, the amount of ground the airborne buck covered was even more incredible. When things calmed I measured

Any apple within seven feet of the ground is ripe for picking by whitetails.

the distance the jumping buck had flown through the air. It was just shy of 30 feet. I've seen a lot of running, jumping and bounding from whitetails in my life but nothing like that scene. It's something I'll never forget.

▶ Heavyweight Contenders

When confronted, whitetails will nearly always attempt to outrun their enemy, be it man or beast. However, there are times when they will choose to stand their ground and confront their opponent. Simply put, they can dodge and weave or stand their ground and duke it out with the best of them. Even the biggest buck has cat-like reflexes that allow him to elude slashing antler tines.

Of course there are times when "attitude bucks" opt to brawl rather than slash and jab when confronted by an adversary. During these confrontations fighting can resemble Greco-Roman wrestling matches, where opponents try to outmuscle each other by pushing and trying to throw each other to the ground. During these skirmishes it's usually a given buck's gift of strength, balance and leverage that wins the day.

▶ Ultimate Survival Machine

In nature there are no gold medals for achievement. An animal's ultimate award is its ability to survive to see another sunrise. For this to happen, whitetails must utilize all of their physical and sensual abilities. Every ability, be it running, jumping, seeing, hearing or smelling, must work together for a whitetail to elude danger. When it comes to surviving, very few animals on planet Earth can stack up to a whitetail. Its speed and jumping ability are legendary, but few outside the hunting fraternity know of its fine-tuned senses.

Sense of smell: One doesn't have to be around whitetails long to realize that they survive more often than not because of their ability to sniff out danger. Of all their senses their sense of smell is the one that impresses me most. Speculation has it that deer can smell anywhere from a hundred to

With a running start a whitetail can easily clear a 25-foot-wide stream.

During the rut, when the wind blows from the south, our research bucks will pace along the facility's south fence line, scenting does on the nearby hillside, which is 425 yards away.

a thousand times better than man. We will probably never know the real number for sure. However, what all deer enthusiasts do know is that a whitetail's sense of smell is remarkable.

By way of example, my whitetail research facility's south fence line is 425 yards from the nearest woods. During the rut, when there is a wind out of the south, my bucks pace the south fence, staring across open space toward the woods where wild deer are bedded. As they stand statuesque they often sniff and test the wind coming from the woods' direction. This reveals two things: they can

Whitetail bucks are among the most aggressive fighters in the animal kingdom. Their agility, strength and fighting ability are showcased when a fight breaks out between two mature bucks.

When irritated, dominant does will attack a mature buck.

smell other deer at least 425 yards away and bucks can sift through all kinds of odors to pick up the smell of an estrous doe. That's impressive!

Eyesight: Whitetails may not possess the eyes of birds of prey, but you should never assume they cannot see as well as humans. Research done at the University of Georgia has shown that deer don't have the same optic cellular structure as people but they certainly have the rod/cone cell makeup to suggest they can see certain colors. Specifically, blue and yellow colors can most likely be seen by deer. Because deer see very well into the blue wavelength of light, they are able to see extremely well in dim light. So their nighttime vision is very good, equipping them with the ability to survive predation any time of the day or night.

Hearing: Though a whitetail's hearing ability doesn't get as much attention as its ability to smell, it should. Time and time again, I've witnessed the whitetail's unbelievable hearing. It's been my experience that deer's ability to hear far exceeds that of a human.

This is better understood through the writings of noted whitetail expert Leonard Lee Rue III, who summarizes the whitetail's ability to hear as follows: "The auditory canal openings in deer and humans are the same size, about one-third inch in diameter, but a

deer's much larger ear allows more sound waves to be picked up and funneled into the ear opening.

"Another advantage that deer have is that their range of hearing is much wider than humans'. Most human adults can hear frequencies in the range of 40 to 16,000 cycles per second. Deer can hear frequencies as high as 30,000 cycles and perhaps beyond. I often use a 'silent' dog whistle while doing photography, to get a deer's attention and cause it to look at me alertly. These devices have been machine tested to 30,000 cycles, and although humans can't hear them, dogs and deer respond readily."

When you put together all the physical attributes a whitetail possesses, is it any wonder that they can survive unlike few animals on earth? They are incredible creatures and in spite of the many advances in hunting technology over the last 20 years, man is still at a disadvantage when it comes to outsmarting a whitetail.

Whitetails wherever they are found are the real deal, ultimate survivors. Their athleticism and physical attributes have allowed them to outmaneuver and outsmart the cagiest creatures for centuries, and this will no doubt be the case until the end of time. As you will see in the coming chapters, they truly are nature's superstar.

Talk about being double-jointed! This buck effortlessly grooms his flank.

CHAPTER 2

Lovers and Fighters

I'd been perched high in a hemlock tree since dawn, waiting patiently at an intersection of two well-used runways. Action was slow. Rather than being entertained by buck activity, my entertainment was fluttering chickadees and scampering gray squirrels. In spite of the inaction, I was committed to sticking it out as long as I could. The rubs and scrapes in the vicinity of my stand told me "this is where the action is."

Two hours into my vigil, chickadees and squirrels were interrupted by what sounded like deer running in the creek below. The 100 yards that separated me from the water made it hard to know exactly what was going on but I suspected that a rutting buck was chasing a "hot" doe. For the next 20 minutes I strained to see what was making all the noise.

The sounds of grunts and branches breaking were getting louder, but the forest was so thick that I couldn't see the deer. Quickly I removed my bow from its rest and prepared for action.

Within minutes of birth a fawn will begin to explore its surroundings. At birth a fawn weighs six to nine pounds.

A doe exploded up the trail and stopped 20 yards away in a thick blowdown. She was panting heavily and looking back over her shoulder. It was obvious a buck was hounding her. Within seconds I heard three short grunts, and then the buck came into view. The heavy racked eight-pointer was soaking wet from running in the creek. Unfortunately, before he got to one of my shooting lanes he veered off the trail, circling the doe as she stared intently at him.

I was so focused on the buck and doe that I didn't realize another deer was close by. With the buck and doe in a standoff I heard a branch break behind me. Fearing the buck and doe would spot me, I tried to remain motionless. With each passing second the suspense built. Finally it was too much to bear. Slowly I turned my head to look behind me. I couldn't believe my eyes. Not 20 yards away a second big buck stood statuesque. He was looking right past me at the big eight-pointer and doe.

For the next minute the forest was dead quiet. Nothing moved and I was sure one of the deer would hear my heart pounding inside my chest. The buck behind me took a step in the direction of the buck and doe but stopped abruptly when the big eight-pointer shouted at him with a loud snort-wheeze. It was if he was saying, "You come one step closer and I'll kill you."

With bucks on each side of her the doe squeezed into the thick tangle of treetops and bedded. I'd seen her behavior enough times in my career to know that she was in estrous and wasn't going to run. It was clear that breeding rights were about to be sorted out.

The big eight-pointer went on the offensive. He jumped a big log and headed toward the buck that was behind me. The commotion that followed was deafening. Through the maze of hemlock branches under my stand I could see the two big bucks come together. The noise they made was explosive. For

A doe's bond of love and nurturing begins at birth. For the first sixty days of a fawn's life its mother protects, cares and feed them 24/7.

the next minute, amidst the sound of breaking branches and bellowing grunts their fight raged. Then, as fast as it began it was over when the intruder buck broke and ran from the big eight-pointer.

In one motion the big buck turned end for end and headed back to where the doe had been bedded. She was gone. During the fight the doe had bolted, without the deer or me noticing. The big buck took up her track and disappeared. Neither buck presented me with a shot, but the memory of their show has remained etched in my mind for nearly a quarter century.

▶ Similar Traits

For over 30 years I've lugged bow, gun and camera across North America in pursuit of whitetails. It has been an incredible journey. And now that I've taken thousands of photos of white-tailed deer, one thing is crystal clear: Whitetails truly are lovers and fighters. Except

Four to five times a day a doe will nurse her fawn. By way of comparison, a whitetail's highly nutritious milk is approximately 10% fat, while a dairy cow's milk contains roughly 2% to 4% fat.

Just before birthing, a doe will fight vigorously for territorial rights to where she wants to give birth. I took this photo a mere 75 yards from where I found the doe's newborn fawn the following morning.

for the lure of food few things dominate a whitetail's life quite like their bonding process (both buck and does) and the competition ritual they go through to ensure that the species survives.

The love that does have for their young is very similar to a human mother's love for her children. The interaction between whitetail bucks is not that much different from behavior exhibited by many human males. Though some people may struggle with such analogies, it's clear to me that God had an impressive blueprint, parts of which are shared by many species in His creation.

▶ The Love Machine

Does: Few things happen until something is taught in our society. The same can be said when it comes to whitetails. In a deer's case teaching begins at birth. Certainly instincts play a part in animal development but the way a whitetail doe cares for her offspring plays a huge role in determining the animal they will become.

Nursing, grooming, protecting and teaching dominate a doe's existence for the first sixty days of a fawn's life. During this time the doe will seldom be far from her fawns. It's a learning process that ensures her offspring know how to survive in a predator-filled world.

Not only are does affectionately protective of their fawns but they are also stern disciplinarians. Nature is often cruel and without does setting limits on what their fawns can and cannot do, many would surely die before their time. Does can be harsh with their fawns and seldom "spare the rod" when it comes to teaching them how to survive.

I once observed a doe that was having a difficult time keeping her young fawn from following her after feeding time. Each time the doe attempted to leave after feeding the fawn it would try to follow her. Finally the doe whacked the fawn several times with her front foot to communicate her desires. The doe's "child abuse" wasn't pretty but it was effective. It got the fawn to bed in thick protective

During summer, with testosterone at a low ebb, adult bucks will often tolerate each other enough to groom each other. I've seen such grooming go on for up to five minutes.

When in velvet, bucks will usually fight with their hooves.

cover so predators would not find it.

A doe's love game is not confined to just fawns. When does make up a doe family group, much bonding and grooming take place among females throughout the year. This is especially so between a doe and her daughters from previous years.

Bucks: Whether or not bucks have a desire to show friendship toward other bucks is open to debate. Certainly their affection is far different from does'. Any bonding or friendship a buck shows toward another buck or group of bucks is confined to season. It is also based on the hierarchy of the bachelor group a given buck is a part of.

In late winter and during the summer months when antlers are growing, several bucks will often form a bachelor group. During this time older bucks may groom each other, but usually such behavior is confined to younger bucks grooming with older ones or visa versa. Even when bucks hang out in bachelor groups the rule of the day is more of

tolerance than affection. It has been my experience that the relationship bucks have with each other is based more on their individual personalities than anything else.

The Rut: For the majority of the year bucks show little interest in does. Unless they share a common feeding area (like a food plot or agricultural fields) they stay segregated. As October inches toward November bucks begin having an interest in does. With the onset of cooler, shorter days bucks expand their territory, going from doe group to doe group in search of an estrous doe. When a buck encounters an interesting doe he's seldom gentle. Rather, he can be quite uncouth in the way he treats his potential lover, often chasing her around in a helter-skelter manner. Once the rut becomes full-blown and the breeding phase explodes, pair-bonding brings does and bucks together for the breeding ritual.

For roughly 24 hours before and after the

Fighting isn't limited to only bucks. Does often fight other does over everything from food to territorial rights.

24-hour estrus period, the scent emitted by an estrous doe causes much attention, especially if the antlered-buck to adult-doe-ratio is balanced. During this magical 72 hours, pair-bonding, chasing and breeding dominate the setting. Throughout the breeding period the dominant buck will move only when the doe chooses to do so. Because does have a tendency to move around much less than bucks, deer activity during the rut's breeding phase can leave a person with the impression that everything in the deer's world has come to a grinding halt.

▶ Don't Mess with Me!

Bucks: A buck's personality goes a long way in determining the kind of lover and fighter he is. After years of observing and raising deer I've come to realize that each deer has a different capacity for loving and fighting. When it comes time to decide who will be king of the forest, the bucks with the biggest head gear don't always rule their territory.

Certainly a buck's age and antler size play a part in determining dominance – but they are not the most important factors.

I'm of the opinion that a buck's personality, his health and the level of testosterone flowing through his body are the driving forces that determine his will to fight once he reaches maturity. These three things shape a buck's attitude. In more cases than not, I've seen four- to six-year-old bucks with respectable head gear (who were jacked up on more testosterone than they knew what to do with) outmuscle, outbluff and outfight bucks who carried Boone and Crockett-size antlers. In nearly a half century of observing whitetails up close and personal I've noticed that the biggest racked bucks are seldom the alpha bucks. In the majority of cases, the mature buck with a body to match his bad attitude is "the man."

When bucks are not carrying hard antlers, most of their fighting takes place via harsh vocalization,

Attitude means a lot in the whitetail population. Once velvet is peeled a buck often thinks he can rule the world. This buck is exhibiting a threat walk as it tries to show its dominance.

body language such as threat walking (where a buck will pull his ears back, bristle up and walk around or toward his adversary) and hoof-to-hoof combat. It can be almost humorous to see the way bucks sometimes try to box with each other as they stand on their hind legs.

Once velvet peels in early fall, hoof-to-hoof skirmishes all but cease. Sparring, harsh vocalization and threat walks are common during the days leading up to and including the rut. It's all part of forming dominance.

When testosterone peaks near the end of October anything can happen in a buck's world and the end result is almost always negative. Though death from antler to antler fighting is not the norm, bruises, puncture wounds and eye damage certainly are. Bucks maxed out on testosterone have been known to chase raccoons, people, vehicles and even trains. They never fare well from their fighting behavior and most skirmishes leave them with lasting scars.

Does: Don't think for a moment that does are not fighters. They are great fighters in their own right, and many know how to box like heavyweight champs. On numerous occasions I've seen mature does flail bucks that ventured too close to their fawns or tried to intrude on their feeding session.

A doe's attitude might be the most aggressive just prior to birthing. Does have preferences for where they birth their fawns. If their offspring from the year before or other deer hang around their turf they will chase them off. It's an incredible thing to observe and shows how serious a doe can be when she needs to be.

The love/fight behavior of whitetails is a beautiful thing to behold. Such behavior is a year-round event that can teach all hunters much about whitetails as they go from birth to death.

Game on! When the rut goes hot-to-trot, fights between two bucks can be life-threatening. Such fights seldom last longer than five minutes but during this time severe physical damage can occur.

Sparring is learned at a very early age. Here a button buck spars with a mature buck. I took this photo in late December. The "bout" lasted about five minutes and ended when the mature buck got up and walked off.

Anatomy of the Rut

In November of 1964 I experienced my first real opening day in the whitetail woods. After being a "designated driver" for the better part of 10 years I was finally old enough to carry a gun to hunt deer, rather than being a gunless driver for my father and other local hunters. By the time my first deer season arrived I thought I knew a lot about whitetail behavior. I didn't. During my youth, I viewed the rut as one frenzied two-week period in the whitetail's life. After 40+ years of extensive hunting and photography, I now realize the whitetail's rut is more complex than I originally thought.

Understanding whitetails during autumn, especially as it relates to the rut, requires knowledge of deer behavior and what triggers the rut's various phases. Everything that precedes breeding – velvet peeling, rubbing, scraping, chasing and fighting – has a purpose. No aspect of the rut is an isolated occurrence. All the activities blend to create one of the nature's most incredible spectacles.

Once velvet peels a buck's testosterone level begins to rapidly rise, triggering the onset of rutting behavior.

During early autumn bucks bed and feed a great deal. For the most part they are visible only on the fringe of daylight.

▶ The Rut's Beginnings

Photoperiodism, the behavioral and physiological responses to changing amounts of daylight, drives nature's timetable, from leaves growing on trees to antlers growing on deer. Though summer's growing season is leisurely for whitetails, subtle changes within the buck population shape a herd's pecking order for fall. Dominant bucks engage in stare-downs, shadowing and, in some cases, flailing with their hoofs. These behaviors help determine which buck could become the bull of the woods when the breeding game begins.

Nature does not load bucks with their full arsenal before the precise time each weapon is needed. Can you imagine what the woods would be like if a buck's testosterone level peaked in early September rather than the first of November?

By late August, bucks' velvet dries, cracks and peels. About the same time, just enough testosterone surges through their system to inspire rubbing. Then, near the end of September, the testosterone "valve" opens wider, stimulating scraping.

By mid-October, with the days cooler and testosterone levels higher, bucks move more during daylight. Does' estrogen levels start to climb, and they begin to smell different. By early November, bucks' testosterone levels and does' estrogen levels have peaked, setting the stage for what deer hunters call the rut.

▶ Defining the Rut

When someone mentions pre-rut, rut or post-rut to me, I always ask them to explain what those terms mean to me so I can best answer their question. Those terms have been used so many ways over the past 50 years that it's difficult to define them universally.

For biologists and researchers, pre-rut usually defines all behaviors that occur before full-blown breeding. In contrast, most hunters think of the pre-rut as the early autumn period when days are warm and little rubbing, scraping or fighting occurs.

To researchers, the word "rut" usually means the actual breeding period. But most hunters think it means that much and more, namely the time bucks are going

This is whitetail country! By the time the last leaves fall from the trees the stage is set for the rut to begin in the north.

bonkers while rubbing, scraping, chasing and fighting.

Hunters and biologists agree the post-rut is the period and behavior associated with the time after breeding ends. So the mere study and use of these words is confusing. Although I believe pre-rut, rut and post-rut are good ways to describe a whitetail's autumn behavior, I also believe it is important to break it down more precisely to fully understand what the rut is all about.

▶ Determining Pecking Order

Dominance among white-tailed deer is progressive and ever-changing. By the time a buck's velvet peels, he begins the physical training for his greatest endeavor – breeding. Due to my life-long involvement in athletics this period reminds me of an athlete's preseason training regimen. By late August a buck's physical features are in transition. He's gaining weight but has yet to fully show the effects of testosterone. He is far different from what he will look like by October 1.

Once velvet is peeled in early September, a buck begins to rub more frequently as day length decreases. In the process rubbing allows a buck to leave behind his

scent and visual markers, a way to alert all deer of his presence.

With ever-increasing testosterone in its system, a buck adds another dimension to his identity by making scrapes. Scraping, like rubbing, allows a buck to make his presence known by dispensing scent throughout his area.

Hunters debate whether scraping is primarily a "buck thing" or if it's done to attract does. During my years of photographing and hunting whitetails throughout North America, I've seen many does work a scrape's licking branch. Only twice have I actually seen a doe paw the ground below the licking branch after scenting the licking branch. However, I have killed several does in archery season that were working a scrape's licking branch when I released the arrow. On the other hand I've seen and photographed hundreds of bucks making scrapes during my career. So, based on this, it's my view that scraping is a buck behavior, a behavior they use to dispense scent and show dominance.

I believe scraping is also a satisfying, conditioned response for bucks. When working an overhanging licking branch, a buck is greatly satisfied by the branch

With each passing day, bucks exhibit more rutting behavior. Rubbing increases as the full blown rut approaches. Rubs are a means for bucks to leave their scent and alert other deer to the maker's presence. It's a buck's calling card.

massaging its forehead, preorbital and nasal glands. I don't believe a buck consciously knows it is spreading its scent to other deer.

Judging from the hundreds of photos I've taken of scraping bucks, it appears the satisfying and stimulating aspects of scraping might explain why a buck performs the behaviors so frequently. I'm not

saying scent-depositing isn't a big part of scraping, because it is. But I'm convinced the dynamics of scraping are incredibly complex and serve several functions, probably more than we'll ever realize.

▶ Physical Competition

With rubbing and scraping comes physical

competition. Once free of velvet, most bucks ramp up their aggression through body language and sparring. Sparring is a way for bucks to test the herd's competitive waters. For the most part, sparring matches are playful skirmishes between two bucks of near equal size and stature. However, on occasion, sparring gets out of hand and becomes ugly. The best analogy I can offer is two teen-age brothers playfully wrestling on the living-room floor. Before they realize it, one gets his nose bloodied and tempers flare. Many times while photographing in fall, I've seen sparring matches between bucks follow a similar pattern.

As breeding time nears a buck's hormones are raging, so trouble often befalls a traveling buck. A buck's range frequently expands from about 600 acres in summer to 4,000 or more acres by early November. During this time a whitetail's summer and early fall pecking order falls apart. Because strange bucks continually trespass on each other's turf, chaos invades the whitetail's world.

By the end of October, scraping behavior is near its peak for bucks in the North. When working a scrape's overhanging licking branch, a buck deposits scent from his nasal, preorbital and forehead gland on the branch. Like rubbing, this behavior telegraphs a buck's presence to other deer in the area.

Though scraping behavior is primarily a "buck thing," I've photographed and killed several does that were leaving scent on a scrape's licking branch.

▶ The Seeking Phase

Bucks are more vocal in autumn than at any other time of the year. By November, bucks communicate with other deer by emitting grunts, bleats, snorts, wheezes and snort-wheezes.

With maximum levels of testosterone now flowing, bucks begin cruising from doe group to doe group, looking for an estrous doe. Their noses dictate when and where they go. No doe group is safe as bucks weave back and forth throughout their expanded territory. At this time, all the dynamics of buck behavior unite. Bucks are now finely tuned physical specimens, spending nearly every waking hour rubbing, scraping and looking for does. Judging from research I've conducted for several years, an active buck may make six to 12 scrapes per hour during this rut phase. The frequency depends on how sexually active a given buck is. Every buck in the woods has a different sexual barometer – just like men.

At this time, bucks also lip-curl (a behavior scientists call Flehmening) far more than in previous months. They exhibit this behavior when they find a place where a doe has urinated.

It is believed that lip-curling allows a buck to determine if a doe is entering estrus. The buck traps scent from a doe's urine in its nose and mouth, and then lip-curls. This helps the buck's scent-analyzing device, the vomero-nasal gland in the roof of its mouth, to pinpoint the doe's status.

When a mature buck or an aggressive yearling buck encounters a stranger or a recognized contender, one or two things usually occur. Stare-downs or shadowing usually occur first. It's generally a buck's antlers, body size and attitude that cause an antagonist to cut short the encounter by shying away. Most bucks are aware of the size of their antlers and body and can quickly size up the situation. However, if two bucks of similar size – with testosterone-injected attitudes to match – find each other, the results may get ugly in a hurry.

If a fight to the death begins, the scene becomes spectacular and there are no rules of engagement. Anything goes. A buck's objective is to knock his opponent to the ground, and then stick his antlers into the opponent's body. Such fights can be gruesome, and when it's over, victor and loser alike often need time to recover before resuming their pursuit of does. Combatants sometimes die from their wounds.

Of all the times to hunt, the seeking phase is one of the best times for the stand hunter to be in the woods, especially if the temperature is at or below the norm. The peak of this period is usually three days either side of the rutting moon (see Chapter 8). During this time, bucks are on the move, taking an inventory of sorts of the doe groups in their area. In most cases they will not chase the does they encounter. When the seeking phase of the rut arrives a buck's movement patterns through funnels and along scrape and rub lines are more predictable. Unfortunately, the seeking phase only lasts a short time before blending into the chase phase.

▶The Chase Phase

The chase phase often gets confused with the seeking phase. The two behavior periods overlap, but they're different. The primary difference between the seeking and chasing phase is intensity. For this reason hunters should try to stay in the woods all day during the chase phase because bucks will show any time from sunup to sundown.

This phase usually begins a couple days after the rutting moon and lasts three to four days into the full-blown breeding phase. During the chase phase, does are almost entering estrus, and bucks are frantically trying to be the first to find them. Now a buck will chase every doe it encounters. Such meetings often resemble a cutting horse and rider trying to cut a calf out of a herd of cattle.

Throughout this phase a buck is persistent, knowing it will eventually find a doe that won't run. During the chase phase, scraping and rubbing will continue, and in many cases can be intense, especially in a fine-tuned deer herd. The chase phase often brings more intense fights, especially if two aggressive bucks pursue the same doe.

The chase phase is a great time to hunt, but it often gets frustrating because the action can take bucks out of range of a stand hunter when bucks chase does away from the anticipated kill area.

▶The Breeding Phase

This is the stage that gives the rut its name. When a doe finally enters estrus, she will accept a buck's company wherever she goes. In many parts of North America, the doe-to-buck ratios are so weighted toward females that all available bucks can easily find a hot doe. When breeding begins, scraping nearly ceases and bucks curtail much of the activity that took place throughout the rut's dominance, seeking and chasing phases.

This phase usually begins four to seven days after the rutting moon and lasts for roughly two weeks in a fine-tuned herd. During this time 70% to 80% of the mature does will be bred.

When a buck encounters an estrous doe he will stay with her for up to 72 hours. For the first 24 hours or so, a doe will smell right, but won't be ready to breed. During the second 24 hours, the doe will be in full estrus and allow the buck to breed her several times.

When a doe enters estrus, a buck will bond with her for nearly 72 hours. During the roughly 24-hour period she is in estrus, the dominant buck will breed her multiple times.

When the rut becomes full-blown, some bucks will cover up to 4,000 acres. This creates many encounters with unknown bucks, which sometimes result in fights.

Then, because she continues to smell right for the last 12 to 24 hours, the buck will continue to stay with her.

During those three days, a buck will move only when the doe moves. Because most does cover little ground, deer activity seems to halt during the rut's breeding phase. Only when the doe cycles out of estrus will the buck move on to look for another estrous doe.

The first doe to come into estrus will often cause a commotion by attracting several bucks. When that happens, a dominant breeder buck never rests as he tries to run off all intruder bucks in order to stay in position to breed the doe. Because they have no time to rest or eat, breeder bucks may lose up to 25% of their pre-rut weight during the rut's seeking, chasing and breeding phases.

Of all the rut's phases, the breeding time can be the most difficult to hunt because of the doe's limited movement patterns. At this time, about the only way tree-stand hunters will see action is to place their stands in areas frequented by doe groups.

▶ Post-Rut – The Recovery Time

By the time a whitetail's prime breeding period ends, a buck's testosterone level is plummeting. A breeder buck is also so rut-worn from the rut's "marathon" that its body is in near meltdown. Whitetail behaviorists have been able to observe that whitetail bucks often crash for a few days once the prime

breeding is complete, much the same way world-class marathoners do after having run a sub-three-hour marathon. They are so exhausted that they may hole up for several days during this time. This is a trait/phase that I've observed and photographed for the last 15 years through extensive photography and raising deer.

Researchers have found that some bucks are so worn down by the time breeding is over that they'll have trouble surviving a hard winter. With less testosterone to drive them, bucks go into a resting and feeding mode as soon as the breeding ceases. In regions of high adult doe-to-antlered-buck ratios, the stress of an extended breeding season decreases the survival chances of many breeder bucks, especially where heavy snow and cold are common.

Even with does entering estrus at nontraditional times, such as December and January, the rutting behavior of bucks will not be as intense as it was in the prime rut. Limited, subdued chasing will occur, but scraping and serious fighting is mostly over. Most post-rut rutting behavior is done by subordinate bucks in the form of sparring, but minor scraping and rubbing will likely occur.

Survival again becomes more important than breeding. The post-rut is a time for bucks to restore fat and energy reserves, for most bucks seem to know their only chance of surviving a Northern winter is to rest and feed heavily.

Lip curling – a behavior scientists call "Flehmening" – is believed to let a buck know if a doe is in estrus.

CHAPTER 4

When the Rut Goes Bonkers

Contrary to popular belief, the whitetail's rut is not a 100-yard dash to the finish line. It is more like a marathon where the contestants run along at a brisk pace for 26 miles or more. In a fine-tuned deer herd the rut's length will be approximately 40 days long. Along the way the seeking phase blends to the chase phase before climaxing in the breeding phase.

During the seeking and chasing phase of the rut there will be ebbs in behavior when action is slow. However, when the chase phase begins blending into the breeding phase emotions often run high in the buck population. During this time only a few does are in estrus, so bucks can often out number estrous does by a large margin. This sets the stage for chaotic breeding parties to form. With several bucks vying for breeding rights, the woods explode.

The day begins with dominant buck bedded with estrous doe.

▶ Anatomy of a Breeding Party

The chasing, fighting, vocalization, rubbing, scraping and breeding that occur within a whitetail breeding party can be incredible when several bucks attempt to breed the same doe. From the time one or more bucks locate an estrous doe until she cycles out of estrus can occur one of the more spectacular events in the wild. In the majority of cases the physical toll that the breeding ritual puts on the buck population is amazing.

Over the course of my career I've witnessed and photographed many breeding parties in the deer woods. This chapter chronicles one such breeding party I captured on film in the last couple years ago.

▶ A Magic Day

Dawn broke cold, overcast and spitting snow, quite typical for November in the North. Only the gurgle of the nearby stream was audible to the big dominant buck. For the better part of the previous two hours he had drifted in and out of

sleep while bedded a few yards from a near-estrous doe. Every now and then he looked to his right, spying his competition. Less than 50 yards away lay two other 10-pointers. It was obvious that neither had the headgear or attitude to compete with the dominant buck. In mere days, when the majority of does would begin cycling into estrus, these bucks would each have their own does to court and breed. However, with breeding just beginning they found themselves playing second fiddle to the big buck.

Throughout most of the night the doe had avoided the dominant buck's every advance. Several times under the cover of darkness the big buck chased off subordinate bucks when they got too close to the doe. Now, overcome with the urge to breed, the doe was beginning to warm to the big buck and was less wary of his sexual advances.

An hour into daylight, the bedded doe and bucks were alerted by the sound of water splashing and rocks clattering in the stream below. Something was crossing the stream and coming their way. All

The breeding party of subordinate bucks jump the bedded doe and begin chasing her, with dominant buck in tow.

Once the dominant buck catches the doe and subordinate bucks, the chase intensifies with the dominant buck chasing the doe.

Once the chase is done the dominant buck and estrous doe try to catch their breath.

craned their necks intently to see what was making the noise. Through the tangle of ground hemlocks two bucks emerged, halted 30 yards away and surveyed the bedded group.

The dominant buck quickly glanced at the doe before emitting a long drawn-out wheeze. One of the incoming bucks, a 10-pointer, grunted, lowered his head and broke for the doe in a classic bird-dog trot. The party was heating up!

Sensing chaos in the making, the doe jumped to her feet and bolted off through the hardwood forest with the lovesick 10-pointer in hot pursuit. In an instant, the other bucks sprang into motion and followed. The chase was on.

For 200 yards the doe led the five bucks on a mad dash through a tangle of blow downs before entering an open field. After a brief chase back and forth across the field the entire party reentered the woods and descended into a deep ravine. With leaves flying in her wake, the doe reached a small stream. In a single bound she cleared the 15-foot-wide swath of moving water. Rather than jumping the stream, the big dominant buck and smaller 10-

pointer hit the water in mid-stride. Water sprayed in every direction as the bucks exited the stream and scampered up the stream's bank, frantically looking for the doe. They didn't have to go far.

Deciding she couldn't outrun the caravan of bucks, the doe stopped near a thick deadfall at the edge of a small clearing. Her chest heaved as she struggled to breathe. Next to her the dominant buck paced back and forth, guarding her from the four intruders who stood motionless, gasping for air, less than forty yards away. The chess match was full-blown and it was anyone's guess who would make the next move.

The big dominant buck took the initiative. Not liking what he saw he vocalized with a loud snort-wheeze before charging one of the 10-pointers. The subordinate 10-pointer whirled and ran. The dominant buck immediately stopped and fired off two loud snorts. He was furious!

Forty yards away one of the other breeding party bucks, sensing the crowd was too large, decided to pare down the competition. The buck bristled up, and began walking stiff-legged toward

While the dominant buck is near the doe a subordinate buck attempts to get close to the doe and a fight breaks out. After a brief tussle the subordinate buck breaks and runs off.

After the fight the dominant buck goes back to the estrous doe and attempts to threaten the subordinate bucks who are stalking the doe. He does this with aggressive vocalization and bluff charges.

another of the breeding party bucks. Standing at the doe's side, the big dominant buck watched to see how the pecking order would shake out. As the two bucks shadowed each other another of the breeding party's bucks moved in on the doe, exhibiting the classic bird-dog trot as he approached. Light snow was now beginning to fall as the dominant buck whirled and ran to head off the intruding buck. A fight was imminent.

At the field's edge the two bucks came together. For 30 seconds they fought fiercely before the lesser buck broke and ran. As quickly as the fight started it was over.

While the brief skirmish was taking place, the doe ran into the woods. Once the fight ended it only took a few moments before all the bucks caught up and surrounded her. For the next half-hour the dominant buck paced back and forth near the doe. Throughout this time he vocalized with snorts and wheezes, attempting to keep the other bucks at bay. With all five bucks less than 50 yards away, the doe bedded in the safety of a tangled blowdown.

With the estrous doe protected by a cocoon of logs the dominant buck challenged each of the subordinate bucks. When none of his aggressive snort-wheezes managed to get the bucks to give ground he reverted to bluff-charges. As if to tease,

one of the subordinate bucks began to make a rub 35 yards away. The dominant buck responded by making one of his own, only yards from the bedded doe. For the next five minutes the two bucks attempted to outrub each other. All this time the other three bucks watched intently from striking distance. Then, one by one, each buck bedded and the woods returned to calm. Mid-day arrived. In spite of all the aggressive rutting behavior taking place, no breeding occurred.

▶ Dash to the Finish

For the next two hours time stood still. Other than a casual glance the bedded doe paid little attention to any of the bedded bucks that surrounded her. Occasionally the dominant buck, who was bedded closest to the doe, closed his eyes and dozed, only to be become alert again when he thought one of the four bedded bucks was about to make a move on the doe.

As the afternoon began to fade the doe stood up, urinated and moved toward the field's edge. After quickly surveying the other bucks the dominant buck slowly rose and stretched before walking to where the doe had been bedded. He smelled the doe's bed for a few moments before lifting his head and turning his nose into the southwest breeze. For the

The estrous doe beds. With all the bucks within a short distance of the doe one of the subordinate bucks begins to make a rub. Not to be outdone, the dominant buck follows suit and begins rubbing a tree next to him. This show of aggression is an attempt to show the subordinate buck who is boss.

next half minute he lip-curled before licking his nose and walking off to follow the doe. Quickly, one of the lesser 10-pointers rose and walked to where the doe had been bedded, smelled her bed, and, like the dominant buck, lip-curled. As the doe disappeared from sight the other bucks got up and headed for the field.

By the time all the bucks had reached the wood's edge the doe was entering a thick brush lot on the far side of a small clearing. The dominant buck quickly scurried across the opening, pausing at the brush lot's edge to aggressively work an overhanging licking branch. Aside from the branch slapping against antler bone only the sound of the slight breeze flowing through the nearby brush could be heard. With light wet

With tension running high the estrous doe jumps from her bed and moves off. The dominant buck walks to where she had bedded, smells the bed for urine, then lip curls.

snow falling, the breeding party came to another halt.

Slowly, with the other bucks watching, the dominant buck stepped into the thick cover. Though the tightly woven mesh of low growing branches made it difficult for the buck to follow the doe, he eventually found her. It was obvious from the doe's behavior that she felt protected by the jungle of brush. Immersed in the brush lot, the doe remained motionless for the next twenty minutes. The scene was one of utter silence. The calm was too much for one of the subordinate bucks to bear. He could make out the doe standing motionless in the brush and apparently had lost track of where the dominant buck was standing. Because he couldn't see the big buck he made his move on the doe. It turned out to be a move that nearly got him killed.

As soon as the subordinate buck entered the brush

the dominant buck emitted a loud wheeze and began bulldozing his way toward the intruder. The sound of branches whacking against antlers pierced the November cold. In an instant the lesser buck decided to abandon his love march and run for his life. After a momentary struggle to break free of the brush, the subordinate buck found a narrow opening and broke for safety. All that stood in his way was a cattle fence, which he cleared with feet to spare.

Ironically, throughout all the commotion the doe never moved. She was ready to breed. Feeling in total control, the big dominant buck approached the doe and began licking her flank. For the next few moments the two engaged in intimate pair-bonding before the buck mounted and bred her.

Once finished the buck slid off the doe's back and stood beside her for a couple minutes. The other four bucks watched from a distance. Slowly the doe walked 10 yards before bedding in thick cover. As if on cue, the big buck bedded nearby. One by one the four subordinate bucks fanned out and bedded within 50 yards of the dominant buck and doe. Silence returned to the scene. Time passed and nightfall arrived, and the magic day was over.

▶ Epilogue

Though the foregoing is typical of what occurs when a breeding party takes place, I'll be the first to admit that no two are ever the same. Just when you think you've seen it all, something new and exciting happens. That's the way it is in the whitetail's world.

The bottom line is that whitetails are predictably unpredictable. Consequently, few things are ever guaranteed. In the next chapter I'll discuss the various triggers and suppressers that can influence the rut's intensity.

The beauty of the whitetail rut is witnessing the myriad of behaviors and the excitement that unfolds. But the frosting on the cake takes place when you are able to see all the rutting behaviors packaged together in the form of a breeding party. This is when the rut becomes magic.

This subordinate buck attempted to move in on the buck and doe, only to be run off by the aggressive actions of the dominant buck. He is clearly running for his life!

The estrous doe is now ready to breed. The buck smells and licks her flank before mounting and breeding her.

In a matter of seconds the breeding is concluded. During the course of the day I saw the dominant buck breed the doe four more times.

The Hunt

CHAPTERS
FIVE • SIX • SEVEN • EIGHT • NINE
TEN • ELEVEN • TWELVE

CHAPTER 5

Deer Activity

Triggers and Suppressers

Success in the deer woods is dependent on whether deer do or don't move. Without deer movement you quickly become a daydreamer rather than a hunter. It's that simple.

Why deer do or don't move is probably thought about, talked about and written about as much as any topic relating to white-tailed deer. It's a subject that has fascinated me for many years. It certainly keeps avid deer hunters guessing, thinking and oftentimes scratching their head.

I've heard many different theories about deer movement, most of which were soon forgotten. Those I remember were the ones that made me laugh, were profound, or caused me to really think.

Fifteen years ago, after nearly a quarter century in the deer woods, I thought I had a pretty good handle on what influences deer movement. At the time I had read much of what the popular press and scientific community had to say on the subject and felt confident I knew what could or couldn't be expected from whitetails. I should have known better.

When air temperatures rise above the seasonal norm, deer behavior begins to shut down. The warmer the temperature, the less the activity.

Heavy rain can be a temporary suppressor of deer activity. However, once the storm front has passed, activity will return.

The last 15 years of photographing and raising whitetails and being involved in some very interesting research has caused me to rethink some of what I thought to be "gospel" regarding deer movement.

In the broadest sense there are six things that cause whitetails to move or stay on their bellies – weather, hormones, sex ratios, predators (man and beast), food and light (both sun and moon). Though each can trigger or suppress deer activity on its own, it's when they work in concert with one another that they are most noticeable.

▶ Weather

Precipitation. It should be pointed out that unlike humans, whitetails and other wild creatures have built-in mechanisms to alert them of impending weather changes. Whitetails can detect when barometric pressure is falling, even if the sky is clear. They know when conditions are changing and their feeding habits can increase dramatically prior to the arrival of bad weather and after a front has passed.

Through the years I've observed that whitetails typically move more when the barometer is moving, either up or down, than when it is steady. During this time, you'll usually find periods of high humidity with fog, haze, rain or wet snow making up the weather system. When this happens, whitetails become secretive, especially in periods of dense fog. The sudden drop in temperature that often accompanies these fronts doesn't cause whitetails to head for thick cover. Rather, it is caused by the unsettled weather associated with the leading edge of low-pressure fronts. The greatest movement occurs if barometric pressure drops rapidly. With few exceptions, there will be little or no deer movement once the front arrives and the weather becomes nasty. Then as the front passes and the weather returns to normal, whitetails and other wildlife start to move again.

When the storm ends and the barometer rises, deer activity often increases dramatically, provided that air temperatures match the whitetail's comfort zone. Several studies have been completed regarding the effects of barometric pressure on whitetail activity. Illinois biologist Keith Thomas found that greatest whitetail feedings occurred when barometric pressure was between 29.80 and 30.29 inches. When the barometer is falling or rising through this range, deer activity should be greatest.

One of the best times to hunt is immediately after a snowfall. When the storm is over, bucks will be on the move.

Temperature.

Unseasonably warm temperatures shut down deer activity in a heartbeat. Of all activity suppressors, air temperature is perhaps the most powerful influence on daytime deer activity. Other suppressors work with temperature and might sometimes override the influence of temperature on deer movement. However, unless temperature matches a whitetail's comfort zone, movement will halt during daylight hours.

For optimal deer activity during hunting season at the 40th to 45th latitude north, I had always felt that daytime temperatures should not exceed 55° F. My feeling was based primarily on observation, journal notes and selected temperature readings I had kept.

As you will see in Chapter 8, I no longer hold this belief due to a fascinating research project I've been involved in since 1995. One aspect of the research looks at how temperature affects the way deer move. The data has shown a definite decrease in deer movements when daytime air temperature rises above 45° F. It should be noted that this project is being conducted in western New York, at the 42nd latitude. The bottom line is that when air temperature rises above the seasonal norm for a region, deer activity will decrease in direct proportion to how warm it gets.

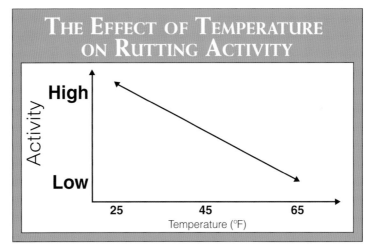

THE EFFECT OF TEMPERATURE ON RUTTING ACTIVITY

Warm weather significantly influences deer movement, especially when temperatures exceed 45° F, north of the 40th latitude.

As autumn's days get shorter a buck's testosterone level increases, triggering a host of rutting behaviors. By the time late October arrives in the North, scraping behavior is near peak.

When the rut goes full-blown, deer activity peaks. During this time bucks are continuously on the move in search of an estrus doe.

By the time October arrives in the North bucks are constantly checking doe groups in an attempt to find one in estrus. Scientists believe that one way they determine this is by lip curling after they've smelled a doe's urine.

Wind Velocity. Down through the years I've heard and read much concerning the impact of wind on deer movements. This coupled with personal observations has made me aware that there are certain times when wind definitely affects deer movement. However, I've never been able to pinpoint what the "magic" wind velocity suppressor is. There have been times when I thought 10 miles per hour was the suppressing point and other times when it was 15 or even 20. The effect of wind on deer movement always seemed to be an elusive ingredient.

It's my belief that the amount of wind velocity required to suppress deer activity has much to do with the region of the country. For example, in prairie states such as Kansas, Nebraska and the Dakotas high winds are a common everyday occurrence, so whitetails in these states don't seem to be as affected by moderate to high winds as they are in the Northeast.

On several occasions I've observed whitetails in Montana and South Dakota freely moving around throughout the day when wind gusts were well over 20 miles per hour. Outside of the hot-to-trot rut, when a buck is chasing other bucks away from his estrous doe, I've seldom seen such a sight in the

Poor adult-doe-to-antlered-buck-ratios can slow down deer activity. The reason is that when there are more than enough does to go around, bucks don't need to be frantically going from doe group to doe group.

part of the Northeast where I live.

Personally I find that it's difficult to determine the wind's impact during the rut because sexually active bucks "throw all caution to the wind" during this time. When a buck's testosterone levels max out and mix with odorous signals from an estrous doe, nothing short of being at ground zero when a bomb goes off seems to stop a rut-crazed buck. However, it should also be pointed out that not all bucks run around helter-skelter during the rut.

It definitely appears that whitetails are affected by higher than normal winds. As with temperature, the key to remember is what takes place when environmental factors are out of the norm for a region of the country. This has been borne out in the research discussed in Chapter 8. By collecting wind data and comparing it to our timer data it is evident that when wind velocity goes much over 12 miles per hour deer movement is suppressed in western New York State – the higher the wind, the less the activity.

It's my firm belief that wind alone doesn't totally shut down whitetails, unless it's gusting over 20 to 25 miles per hour. Rather, it's other factors, such as a rapidly falling barometric pressure or heavy rain or snow, working in concert with the higher than normal wind that cause whitetails to lay low.

Having raised whitetails and spent literally every day for the last ten years around them, I've seen first hand that they rely on their sense of smell more than anything else. When there is too much wind, or wind gusting in irregular patterns, deer don't feel comfortable moving around. Whitetails do one of two things when they are spooky. They either get away from what is making them uneasy or if they know they cannot escape they will hit the ground and wait for conditions to return to normal.

The key to knowing the suppressing effects of wind velocity is being aware of what deer in a given area will tolerate. Here, in western New York, the breaking point appears to be twelve or more miles per hour. It's a regional thing and one all hunters should become aware of.

Human pressure can turn whitetails nocturnal in a heartbeat. Several studies have shown that when man invades the whitetail's world daytime deer activity decreases.

▶ Hormones

Science has revealed how a whitetail buck's hormone levels ebb and flow with changing amounts of daylight (photoperiod).

By the time winter manifests itself, a buck's testosterone level has bottomed out, at which time a separation layer forms at the antler pedicel and the antlers fall off. With hormonal levels at a low point, deer activity slows to a crawl during the winter months.

Then as daylight increases and winter melts into spring, a buck's testosterone level slowly increases and the antlers begin growing again. With warmer temperatures and an abundance of food, deer activity increases dramatically from what it was during the winter months.

Testosterone levels continue to slowly rise throughout the antler-growing season. By early September, a buck's serum androgen levels trigger the velvet-peeling process and the rutting season technically begins.

As the amount of daylight decreases, hormone levels in both bucks and does continue to rise. In the North, the testosterone level in an average buck nearly doubles between October 1 and November 1, before returning to its early October level by December.

Maxed-out on hormones, many bucks will go through the autumn months with a disposition that resembles that of a hyperactive child. Bucks are consumed with the thought of breeding by the time late October and early November arrive and few things will slow them down.

Raging hormones are the driving force behind a buck increasing its range in the autumn months. Throughout the summer, a buck will cover about 600 to 1,000 acres of land. However, during the rut it's not uncommon for a buck to increase his range to 4,000 or more acres.

Hormones are also a primary trigger of the different types of rutting behavior exhibited by a buck. Their stimulating effect can be seen in rubbing, scraping and breeding behaviors. Simply put, bucks will go ballistic when hormone levels are high, and activity will be at a minimum when hormone levels are low.

▶ Adult-Doe-to-Antlered-Buck Ratio

Much has been made of the influence the adult-doe-to-antlered-buck ratio can have on the rut. If you hunt an area that has more than four adult does for every antlered buck, rutting behavior will be light, with little chasing and decreased amounts of rubbing and scraping taking place. If you hunt an area where the ratio is two to three adult does to every antlered buck, there should be a good amount of visible rutting activity. If the ratio is one-to-one, rutting activity – in the form of chasing, fighting, rubbing, and scraping – should be outstanding. And yes, a few places in North America do have more antlered bucks than adult does. In these areas, the rut tends to be unbelievably intense.

Through the years, I've photographed and hunted areas that have the adult-doe-to-antlered-buck ratios I've described. It's been quite an education, and I've learned

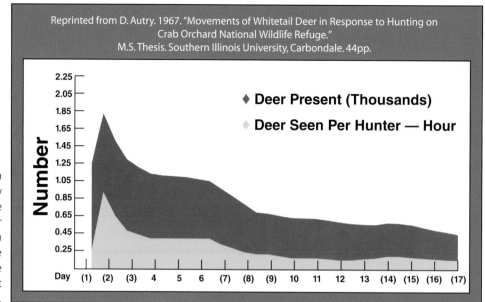

Reprinted from D. Autry. 1967. "Movements of Whitetail Deer in Response to Hunting on Crab Orchard National Wildlife Refuge." M.S. Thesis. Southern Illinois University, Carbondale. 44pp.

This graph illustrates how hunting pressure affects deer sightings. With hunters in the woods, deer move less during daylight hours.

that a tighter adult doe-to-antlered buck ratio almost always creates a more intense rut.

Without competition, there is no need for bucks to go crazy. For this reason, poor ratios suppress rutting activity, night or day, especially in areas where 70% to 90% of the antlered buck harvest is composed of yearlings (1-1/2 year old bucks). This is particularly evident in states where the doe population has been protected at the expense of antlered bucks. When too much pressure is put on bucks, all aspects of the whitetail world suffer, especially rutting behavior.

Another thing that lessens the intensity of rutting activity is the absence of mature bucks. In areas where a deer population has adequate numbers of mature bucks, the rut's intensity is greater in every aspect, from scraping to breeding.

So, if you don't see the rut as predicted, there is a good chance it's because of poor adult-doe-to-antlered-buck ratios and a lack of mature bucks.

▶ Predator Pressure

The effect of human pressure on whitetail movement is of great interest to the deer hunter. In most parts of the country, the whitetail rut occurs during archery season, so human pressure is not as great as during firearms season. However, in more populated areas, human pressure can pose a significant problem. Whitetails quickly learn that darkness is quieter, less threatening,

Whitetails gravitate to food, especially when the barometric pressure is between 29.80 and 30.29 inches. Wherever the primary food source is located, deer behavior will be high.

and has fewer people.

Location and the amount of human pressure can affect daytime deer sightings tremendously. Many urban areas have high deer populations, but unless landowners are feeding deer, the deer are seldom seen. Human noises, whether from automobiles, sirens or children

In the autumn months, corn is highly preferred by whitetails. This high-carbohydrate food source is a whitetail's candy and a prime place to hunt.

playing, keep deer under cover and out of sight until nightfall. This is especially true with mature bucks.

The graph on page 56 from a research project on the Crab Orchard National Wildlife Refuge in Illinois shows what can happen when hunters invade the whitetail's domain. Remember that it's not just hunters that suppress daytime activity. The presence of any human puts whitetails on red alert. This can mean hikers, bird watchers, or hunters.

▶Food

When you think about the various factors that stimulate or suppress whitetail movement, food probably isn't the first thing that comes to mind. It doesn't have the same frenzied effect that weather or hormones have on whitetails, but its influence on deer activity cannot be denied. The availability, quality, and location of a food source can dictate how far deer move and where they bed.

Due to the cyclical nature of mast crops, deer tend to adopt different travel patterns from year to year. Also, changes in the location and types of farm crops can alter whitetail movement. Whitetails are basically nomads – they gravitate to the best food source available within their home range. If drought conditions hit an area, they may even shift their home range.

When an exceptional mast crop is present (e.g., apples, acorns or beechnuts), whitetails move very little because they typically bed right in the food source. In such years, deer that frequent agricultural crops during the summer months shift their attention to the mast when it begins to fall and make little effort to return to the crops before they are harvested. Deer sightings can be hard to come by when this type of scenario exists.

If you want to see the rut's chemistry change, look no further than food sources. The rutting sequence will occur, but you won't see it unless you have prime feeding areas to lure does.

In addition to identifying the food sources whitetails are gravitating to, it's critical to know where they are bedding. Once the bedding area is defined, it becomes much easier to unravel how both bucks and does are moving to and from the most attractive feeding areas.

▶Light

I'll conclude this chapter by mentioning one more trigger/suppressor, the moon –specifically the second full moon after the autumn equinox, which I refer to as the rutting moon. As you will see in Chapter 8, the rutting moon's effect on the rut is quite interesting.

Though much is known about deer behavior, there is no magic answer that explains what stimulates or suppresses movement in the whitetail population. Many factors are responsible, and it's not uncommon for several different variables to work in concert with one another. The more stimuli present at a given time, the more activity you'll witness. On the flip side, more suppressants will result in less activity.

Research has enabled hunters to understand many aspects of deer movement, yet there is still much that remains unexplained. In studying the subject, two things become clear – it is unbelievably complex and incredibly fascinating.

CHAPTER 6

Structure Your Hunt

Athletics have always been a huge part of my life. From a very early age, my life was dominated by baseball and basketball every summer and winter, either as a player, a coach or a referee. Along the way there were many successes and some failures. Winning was great, but it was the failures that made me a better athlete and coach.

Winning strategies don't just happen. To be a consistent success on the hardwood court or ball field requires ability and a game plan to win. And the key to a great game plan is how the plan is structured. Structuring to win requires an understanding of the endeavor, a mastery of the fundamentals, fine tuning through repetition and execution. The same structure required in competitive athletics applies to successful whitetail hunting. The bottom line is that becoming a great whitetail hunter doesn't require the intellect of a rocket scientist. It does, however, require that the hunter understands the animal, the environment it lives in and how to execute a plan. When these three aspects are mastered, success follows.

A whitetail's sense of smell is its greatest defense against danger. Under the right conditions they can easily pick up odors from several hundred yards away.

The key to stand location is its relationship to the prevailing wind. Never place a stand where the wind isn't in your favor.

▶ Understanding the Animal

Over the course of the last 20 years I've written many behavior-related articles for various hunting publications. In nearly every piece I emphasized that having a keen understanding of whitetail behavior is "the ticket to the dance."

The success of so many strategies is tied to how well one knows deer behavior – the more you know the better your chances of structuring and executing a successful hunt. Fifty years ago, when I was just learning about whitetails, there were few if any forms of media to unravel the mysteries of deer behavior. Until the early 1980s the only way one could observe deer behavior was the old-fashioned way, which was in the field. In most cases this required years of study. This is no longer the case. Now there are hundreds of videos that enable hunters to shorten the learning curve. In spite of all the whitetail behavior related items on the market, many hunters still try to take short cuts or force the issue when it comes to outsmarting a buck. Doing so seldom works. One of the biggest mistakes hunters make is trying to overcome what I call ill-wind.

▶ Work the Wind, Beat a Buck

"Scent is the most important sense tied to memory." In so many cases a successful hunt boils down to how well a hunter understands the wind and how to work at keeping a whitetail from smelling him. If you don't have the wind in your favor, you are doomed.

A whitetail truly lives and dies by his or her nose. Their ability to detect predators is legendary. Whether a whitetail's sense of smell is a hundred or a thousand times better than man's may be debatable, but the reality is that they can smell danger far better than we can imagine. We've done many interesting studies at our whitetail research facility over the years. One that was discovered by accident dealt with the distance at which deer can pick up odors.

The southern boundary of our 35-acre enclosure is 425 yards from the nearest woods. During the rut when there is a wind out of the south and does are coming in or in estrous, our bucks will pace or stand next to the southern fence line, staring in the direction of the hillside, raising their noses to pick up scent. Because there is only open space between the fence and the woods we know that whitetails can detect odors from at least 425 yards away. Having observed this, it's my belief that they probably can smell odors at far greater distances. So, to consistently kill whitetails it is critical that hunters understand how air moves.

Wind currents and thermals should be periodically checked while on stand. This can be done with wind floaters or unscented sprays. If the wind current is not in your favor, move to another stand.

How Thermals Work (On calm days) — Morning Thermals — Evening Thermals

Stream

WIND CURRENTS

< West   East >

Steady Winds

Variable Winds

Steady Winds
Variable Winds

Stream

▶ Tracking Air

Thermals: I wish I could count the number of times that thermals have messed up one of my hunts. For the most part thermals are characteristic of how air moves early and late in the day when there is virtually no wind. Typically a calm, cool, sunny morning will cause air to move up a hillside once the sun rises and begins warming the air.

The reverse can take place at the end of the day. On warm sunny days, as the sun inches toward the horizon, cool air will begin dropping back down a hillside. Of course the least little breeze will cause thermals to eddy back and forth, creating yet another obstacle for the hunter. Also, I've found that eddying thermals can be quite common in thick conifer forests or in early season hunting situations, before leaf-off.

Steady wind: Steady wind movement can be both good and bad; it all depends on one's hunting location. For the hunter who hunts in flat country or on ridge tops a steady breeze generally moves consistently in the same direction, without eddying. For this reason such locations will almost always be the best ambush points to hunt when the wind kicks up.

Attempting to hunt on a hillside or in the bottom of a ravine or valley is usually futile when the wind is blowing. This is because as wind passes over a sudden drop in elevation it tends to swirl throughout the lower terrain (ravine or valley). Unfortunately hunters all too often think they might get lucky and catch the wind right when the buck comes by. Think again. Remember the description of how far deer can smell and learn it well. Nine times out of 10 you will not succeed trying to play this game. Deer remember very well. That's why they survive the way they do.

The two best stand locations on our farm are on the side of a ravine and in the ravine's bottom. I learned long ago that neither location can be hunted if there is the slightest hint of a breeze.

Gusty wind: Of all wind conditions, gusty winds are the worst for a stand hunter. Little good can come

Formulate a hunting plan for every situation. Setting up a foolproof strategy is the key to success.

Before setting foot in the woods I study aerial photos and topo maps for the area. By comparing both you can pick up where the travel corridors and food sources are likely to be. Learn how to use both and you'll become a better hunter.

from gusty wind conditions because they tend to create the ultimate eddying effect. This is particularly the case when wind velocities of over 10 mph are broken with brief intervals of calm or decreased wind velocities. When this occurs, scent blows in every direction known to man. In some parts of North America gusty wind conditions also have a tendency to shut down deer activity.

Humidity: The amount of moisture in the air determines how well a deer can smell. If you've ever observed a whitetail up close you will notice that they are continually moistening their noses with their tongues. They do this partly to keep their noses and nostrils moist so scent can be detected more easily. Consequently on damp days (when the humidity is higher) deer will be able to smell better.

▶ Finding a "Honey Hole"

Wind direction should always dictate where you hunt. With that said, there are several set ups that can provide the ultimate "honey hole." What follows is my list, by preference, from a near half-century in the deer woods.

Funnels: I hunt nearly every structure ever written about but my greatest successes have come from hunting funnels, especially thick brushy funnels that are not wind sensitive. When a narrow body of cover attaches a bedding area to a feeding area it becomes a prime candidate for a potentially great

set-up. It is here that you'll find rubs and scrapes when the rut ramps up.

Inside Corners: Inside corners are my second most favorite place to hunt whitetails. What makes inside corners great hunting locations is that a whitetail will usually opt to cut the corner just inside the woods or brush line in order to get from point A to B. This is especially true in areas with high hunting pressure. Also, if there is a prime food source in a field where the inside corner exists, deer will have a tendency to enter the food source at the point of the inside corner.

Ravine Heads: If given a choice, whitetails will go around a ravine before going down and back up, even if it adds a couple hundred yards to their journey. Because of this the head of a ravine or steep draw can be an excellent place to ambush the buck of your dreams when food sources are nearby and the rut is full-blown.

Benches: I grew up hunting benches, which are common in the hilly country of our area of western New York. Some are no wider than 30 yards and some 100 yards wide. The beauty of hunting benches is that they can offer some incredible opportunities (if the wind cooperates) because they allow whitetails to move more freely along a hillside's steep inclines.

Ridge lines: Volumes have been written by whitetail experts on the benefits of hunting along

Funnels and pinch points are my favorite places to hunt. Few locations offer more action, especially when the rut ramps up.

ABOVE: Acorns are one of the whitetail's most preferred foods in the fall. Wherever you find acorns you'll find deer.

LEFT: When a buck works a scrape he almost always offers a standing broadside shot. I usually hang my stand 18 to 20 feet high, 15 yards downwind of the scrape.

ridge lines. In such areas where food is available and the terrain thick the hunting can be great. During the rut bucks are habitual ridge runners because they can cover a lot of ground and detect does at lower elevations through wind currents. Most ridge lines can offer great hunting set ups because wind direction is more predictable.

▶ Build a Whitetail Super Highway

The majority of my rut phase hunting is in funnels or transition zones, those areas deer travel through to go from bedding areas to feeding areas. If conditions and habitat are right, several trails may pass through such areas. The best hunting site is usually near the trail with the most rubbing and scraping sign in mid-

October. If sign is spread throughout the transition zone, you must take several steps to make one trail more attractive than the others.

To make a trail more attractive, I hang two to five mock licking branches along the trail I want to hunt over, spacing them about 50 yards apart. Using plastic draw ties, I attach a mock licking branch on an existing branch, about 5-1/2 feet off the ground. If there is no existing branch over the trail, I attach the mock licking branch to a wire strung between two trees. Once done, I expose the earth below each licking branch, which makes the site look like a natural, active scrape. I've used attractant lures on the branches, but have discovered they're not necessary.

With or without lure bucks usually begin working

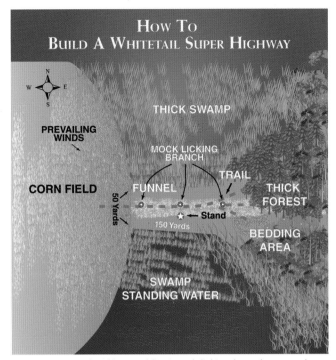

How To
Build A Whitetail Super Highway

This is an example of how adding mock licking branches to a deer trail between a prime bedding and feeding area can make a great setup. Placing mock licking branches every 50 yards along the trail will enhance the trail and make it more attractive for deer usage.

I've made a career of hunting scrape lines in travel corridors. It's not uncommon for sexually active bucks to make over six scrapes every hour they are on their feet.

the mock scrapes within 48 hours. The mock scrape will concentrate deer activity, so be sure to clear a shooting lane that is at least 10 to 15 feet wide.

In November 2001, I shot a beautiful 140-inch Pope and Young buck and two does using this tactic. Last fall, while hunting on our farm, I harvested a 140-class buck as it was about to use one of my mock licking branches. You might be surprised to hear that does work licking branches, but in my experience, nearly all deer work mock licking branches as they walk past, providing you with a clean shot at close range. This is an incredibly effective strategy that I discovered years ago while photographing deer.

▶ Force 'em Past You

For the better part of 30 years I've used the following three methods to force deer past my stand.

1. When multiple trails pass through a funnel you can make one much hotter than another by making the other difficult to travel. Often I'll plug up the funnel's other trails with fallen trees or brush. When other trails are choked off deer will quickly use the open trail.

2. Piling brush can also be used when hunting

over a food plot where you want to force the deer to stay in the food plot and in front of the stand location. By windrowing piles of brush behind and away from your stand you can keep deer from passing behind you where they will wind you.

3. Another way to force a whitetail to go where you want is by erecting a fence line to funnel them past you. Of course you need to own the land or have permission to do so. Over the years I've had success bringing deer past my stand location by building a 5-1/2 feet high wire fence (four-strand unbarbed wire). Some have been 50 yards long, some as long as 100 yards. Rather than jump the fence a buck will opt to walk it and pass right by your stand. Erecting such a fence is actually cheaper than you might think. Unbarbed wire comes in 1,500-foot rolls and sells for less than $25 at farm co-op stores. In most cases the wire can be stapled to small trees.

▶ The Ambush

Once a hunter becomes versed in the nuances of deer behavior and how to hunt various terrains, the stage is set for sealing the deal when the moment of

By hanging mock licking branches every 50 yards along a funnel's trail you can increase the frequency of deer using the trail. Basically you are building a better, more attractive highway for the deer.

It is easy to monitor deer activity at a scrape. Smooth out the scrape's dirt every two or three days to get an idea of the deer using the scrape. It the track is over 2-1/4 inches wide (in the North) you know the deer is a mature buck.

Well-worn trails in a prime funnel often produce a visible rub line.

TOOLS TO IMPROVE YOUR CHANCES

■ *Maps:*

Much has been written about the value of topo maps and how they can aid a hunter. With an understanding of how habitat and terrain affects deer movement a good topo map can help pin-point prime hunting locations. What follows is a listing of topo map sources.
www.myTopo.com • www.maptech.com
www.delorme.com

■ *Weather:*

Becoming a weather watcher is vital for success. One way to do it is through the internet. By logging onto to the National Weather Service site at www.nws.noaa.gov you can monitor the weather for your particular region of the country.

Raking an entrance/exit trail to your stand will help you keep from spooking deer.

truth comes along.

For starters one needs to execute the details. Doing so requires not being heard, seen or smelled by a whitetail. All are tough to master. In order to get to and from stand locations, make each stand's access trail noise-free. To accomplish this, rake a debris-free trail the last hundred yards to the stand. This will eliminate the sound of branches breaking and leaves rustling.

Seldom will I hang a stand higher than 18 to 20 feet. This is my comfort zone and frankly there is no need to go higher when the terrain is flat. On rare occasions I'll go higher when the land is hilly. To keep from being seen, master the art of concealment. This not only requires matching the camo pattern to the surroundings but also camoing the stand site with natural habitat, such as pine boughs, to break up your silhouette.

A whole chapter could be written on tree stand safety. Suffice it to say, no hunter should ever think of climbing into a tree stand without a great safety harness. When I first started hunting out of portable stands I wore only a safety belt. No more. Research has shown that a safety belt doesn't provide enough protection in a fall because in most cases the victim turns upside down with a belt. Though I've never fallen, I work to keep it from happening by wearing a top-of-the-line chest harness. A safety harness is the best piece of equipment a stand

hunter can own. If you love your family you'll wear it every sit.

The scent problem is the toughest obstacle to overcome in winning the whitetail game. But, by understanding of how air moves and utilizing the various scent elimination products available it is possible to come close, providing the wind is in your favor.

Lastly, don't over hunt a location. Next to failing to master the wind, this may be one of the biggest problem hunters face. Why? Because there is always a tendency to push the envelope and hunt a specific stand over and over. Resist the temptation. If the wind isn't right or you've hunted a site two days in a row, consider moving to another stand. Give the location a rest for a day or so. And work to stay sharp while on stand. Hunting whitetails is often hours of flat-time sandwiched around moments of heart-thumping drama. Find ways to stay ready for the drama-moments.

When it comes to deer hunting, chance favors the prepared man. Consistently killing mature bucks requires that preparation be sandwiched around a dose of luck. But one thing is certain—by blending an understanding of deer behavior, interpreting the wind and learning the lay of the land a great game plan can be formulated. The end game is that you just might be in position to kill the buck of your life.

CHAPTER 7

Hunting the Pre-Rut

The rut drives whitetail hunters. For the avid deer hunter, the magic of November (or whenever breeding takes place in your region) inspires dreams of hunting rut-crazed bucks. It's truly a time all deer hunters yearn for. As grand as that time is, hunting during the time just prior to the rut can be just as productive as the rut.

Historically, the whitetail's pre-rut (what hunters often refer to as the early season or October lull) has generated limited interest among deer hunters. Few serious hunters take their vacation in September and early October and many view it as nothing more than a tune-up for November. But with each passing year, more and more hunters realize that whitetails often provide more and better opportunities well before the hot-to-trot rut arrives.

▶Early Autumn Behavior

For the most part, whitetails are very secretive creatures during September and October, especially the mature animals. As September eases into October, the whitetail's thick winter

coat grows in. This heavier fur, coupled with autumn's warm days, causes whitetails to be less active during daylight hours. As a result, most move at the edge of day and feed at night.

During this period, I've observed a phenomenon that I call the calm before the storm. Prior to a buck peeling its velvet, sightings are fairly consistent. However, once they've shed their velvet the bucks – especially mature bucks – go into hiding. This secretive phase lasts until the rut.

Throughout much of their range, bucks seem to curtail their activity drastically during late September and October. It's almost like they are resting up for the rigors of November's rut when they'll be continually on the move. Does, on the other hand, seem to continue their normal movement patterns. With doe sightings high and buck sightings low, hunting the pre-rut period can be very frustrating.

However, there is a bright side to hunting whitetails early in the season. During this time, the bucks are in bachelor groups and it's not uncommon to find several together. I've seen as many as seven bucks walk by my stand during an early season sit. That is definitely a plus when hunting this time of year. A key to remember is that once the rut arrives, group behavior is over.

Unlike the rut, when buck activity can be high throughout the day, deer activity during the pre-rut or early season, can be very sporadic. This is due primarily to unseasonably warm temperatures that are common during this time. It has been my experience that from early September through late October there is far more deer activity during the last two hours of daylight than at any other time from sunup to sundown. For this reason the evening shift will be better to hunt than the first two hours after dawn.

▶ Off-Season Scouting

Scouting during late winter and spring allows me to analyze what took place the preceding season as well as learn about the bucks that survived. I'm

can afford when pursuing early season whitetails is to cause them to become nocturnal.

Deer activity during late September and early October is at low ebb because of the factors already mentioned. Their behavior makes them far more predictable during this time than during the rut. Before the leaves fall, bucks instinctively seem to get ready for the rut and all the activity associated with it. As a result they crave food – lots of it.

Food preference varies across the country, but where I live, in western New York, old apple orchards, stands of oak, beechnuts, corn, clover, alfalfa and fall-planted grain fields offer distinct hotspots for early season whitetails. Field crops and apples are easy to locate, but mast can be a different story. If there is a good acorn crop, some acorns will start falling in late August. Also, I use a good pair of binoculars to scan the tree-tops looking for acorns and beechnuts.

However, not every stand of oaks or every apple orchard is a hotspot. Don't expect to ambush a whitetail coming to feed during the early season unless there is ample cover and available escape routes. If the necessities aren't there, these food sources will only be visited during the night.

▶The Mast Connection

Soft Mast: Next to hunting food plots probably more early season bucks have been killed in or near apple orchards than any other place. During the early-autumn months, deer habitat is in a state of change, and much plant life is stalky and not palatable for deer. Consequently, when apples start falling, whitetails gravitate to them. Over the years, I've surprised more than one buck as he came to gorge on apples.

On occasion, I erect a portable stand in the orchard if a given tree offers good possibilities. However, if many trees in the area are bearing apples, my strategy changes. Where many bearing trees are present, I locate my stand where the deer must pass to get to the orchard. I prefer this type of ambush because once deer get into an orchard, it is nearly impossible to determine which way they will go. Usually a whitetail will gravitate to whichever tree has the most and

also able to scout bedding areas actively to learn more about deer habits. One of the key aspects of scouting the bedding area in late winter is that it eliminates pressuring a buck. This, along with locating the preceding fall's food source, helps determine how to hunt a given buck or area come early fall. Remember, those food sources are your ticket to success during the pre-rut period.

By virtue of raising whitetails I can attest that bucks increase their body weight by up to 25% during the months of September and October. Knowing this, I scout for the whitetail's main food source during late August and early September. Above all I work diligently to stay out of the bedding areas I located the previous winter and spring. The last thing a hunter

By the time autumn is in full bloom whitetails are in prime condition. A buck's body weight at this time of the year is usually 20% to 25% greater than what it will be when the rut ends.

sweetest apples under it on a given day. Normally there will be multiple trails leading into the orchard where a stand can be erected.

In order to get a buck stopped, try hanging a mock licking-branch over the trail. There is a high probability that every deer (does included) that passes by will stop to work the branch with their forehead, preorbital and nasal glands. When they do you'll have a great opportunity to shoot the deer in the heart/lung area while it is stretched out working the branch.

Hard Mast: If the bedding area around a food source is not well defined, deer will come to feed from literally any direction. If this is the case, I'll erect my stand where I find the most sign (heavy mast on the ground and concentrations of droppings) and move my stand accordingly if needed.

When hunting mast areas, I'll also attempt to find a whitetail signpost rub – a tree that is rubbed year after year – or a well-used scrape. Usually, if mast is present, the signpost rub and area around it will

become more and more active as the rut approaches. Such locations are excellent places for hunting and are frequently visited by several bucks during the course of the early season.

▶ Food Plots and Ag Areas – The Candy Store

Clover, alfalfa and early fall grain seedings can be very productive hunting locations before the leaves fall from the trees. Unfortunately, hunting around larger fields presents problems because deer tend to visit them only under the cover of darkness. However, if the area is made up of small food plots that are under an acre in size (which I call hunting plots), deer will work them feverishly the last hour or two of the day or first hour in the morning. Also, it's been my experience that evening hunts will be much more productive than morning during early fall.

If the food source holds, the locations should become better and better as September fades into late

Few hunting locations can rival apple orchards during the pre-rut.

The pre-rut is a favorite time to hunt whitetails. The days are crisp and autumn's splendor is everywhere.

October because bucks begin making scrapes in a more predictable fashion. When these first scrapes are actively worked, a buck's territory is smaller than it will become in late October. As a result, bucks are more predictable when it comes to hitting these scrapes again. Generally, if thick cover presents itself in areas of heavy soft and hard mast, bucks will work scrapes during daylight hours.

Erecting treestands along well used trails leading to the field can provide a good deal of action. In most cases, it is important to hang the stand at least 15 feet high and a minimum of 50 yards inside the cover in order to get action during legal shooting light. If you are not seeing deer with this type of set-up, you'll have to locate closer to the bedding area. To ensure silence getting to and going from the stand, rake the path to the stand with a lawn rake. This allows for a silent approach.

Calling whitetails using a grunt tube is a great way to bring whitetails within shooting range during hunting season.

When acorns and other preferred mast begin falling from the trees deer will abandon most of their summer foods in favor of these high carbohydrate offerings.

Trail hunting in and around food sources is at its best during early season. When I'm hunting a trail, I like to be at least 15 yards off the trail. Being close to the deer run creates a host of problems, the greatest being a deer smelling or seeing you before it steps into range. Also, avoid placing a stand on a curve in the trail where deer can spot you when they come around it.

In order to continue hunting a given area when the wind shifts, I secure two stand locations, one upwind and one downwind of where I think a buck will appear. Because food sources continually change, I'm a big fan of portable treestands. Portables allow for optimum movement within an area without disrupting a buck's habits. Where legal and possible, you should prepare shooting lanes around your stand. After all, it does no good to make all the preparations for a hunt and not be able to shoot when a buck shows up.

▶ To Beat a Buck's Nose

A whitetail can be fooled some of the time, but you'll seldom beat him when it comes to his ability to detect human odors. If you think you can always rely on wind currents whisking your scent away from the kill area, think again. Master whitetail hunters rely heavily on odor elimination strategies. For this reason the best deer hunters I know would never think of hunting the early season without ScentLok clothing and scent eliminator sprays. I utilize both, along with one additional strategy.

If you don't control your breath odor, it doesn't matter what kind of scent precautions you take. Breath odors spook deer as quickly as body and equipment odors. A person exhales 250 liters of breath air into the surrounding environment every hour, and the resulting odor will spook a deer.

Breath odor can be neutralized two ways. Chlorophyll tablets can be purchased in most drug stores and do a good job of neutralizing breath odors. Perhaps an easier way to eliminate foul breath – provided you have apple trees where you hunt – is to carry an apple with you and suck on a chunk of it as you sit in your stand. Apples are nature's toothbrush and will take away unwanted breath odors.

▶ "Fingerprints" Tell the Story

What goes on in whitetail country before the leaves fall from the trees can forecast what will follow. If a scrape is located in an active feeding area, check the condition of the overhanging licking branch to determine its use. Examining the size of tracks in the scrape will also reveal a lot about the size of bucks using a particular area. Research has shown that in the North, if the tracks exceed 2-1/4 inches in width, the animal will weigh more than 175 pounds. If this is the case it's probably a buck 2-1/2 years of age or older. Often, these early scrapes will turn into primary scrapes when the peak of the rut hits in November.

▶ Calling and Rattling

Because whitetails are very social creatures, I rely heavily on calling during the early season. Bucks, particularly yearlings, are very receptive to doe bleats and buck grunts. If I spot a buck that doesn't appear to be coming my way, I'll make two or three doe bleats or buck grunts. Often this is all it takes to bring a buck in close. If it's a yearling buck, I will not use a low guttural grunt (characteristic of a mature buck), because there is a high probability that the sound will spook it. However, I'll use the low guttural grunt if the buck is mature. The key is to have a grunt tube that allows you to make several different vocalizations.

Rattling can work, and often does, for early-season hunters. But unlike the rut, when I rattle loudly and aggressively, my pre-rut rattling technique consists of trying to create the sound of two bucks sparring. As a result, I just tickle the antler tines together from two to five minutes in an attempt to bring a curious buck to my stand.

▶ Be a Weather Watcher

Learning to be a weather watcher will prove to be as important in the early season as it is to know what the deer are eating. Over the years I've become an ardent weather watcher because of what I know it does to a whitetail's feeding habits. The

By the time mid-October arrives in the North rubs will begin showing up. Check them close for they can reveal information about a buck's antler characteristics.

Much can be learned from checking tracks. The track on the left is less than two inches wide and likely made by a doe or yearling buck. The one on the right is 2-1/2 inches wide and made by a mature buck.

Rattling during the pre-rut can be a great strategy. For best results don't rattle aggressively. Rather, try to imitate bucks that are sparring.

One way to get a buck to stop is by emitting a soft grunt.

subject of weather could fill volumes, but basically whitetails are more active during irregular weather patterns. A rapidly falling barometer usually puts whitetails in a feeding frenzy. Therefore, just prior to a storm's arrival will be an excellent time to be overlooking an apple orchard, food plot or stand of oaks. As stated previously, research has shown that feeding is heaviest when the barometric pressure is between 29.8 and 30.29 inches.

Whitetails will also increase their feeding activity after a low-pressure system moves from an area and a high-pressure pattern returns. Once the low-pressure system moves on and the barometer rises, deer might feed heavily for three or four days to catch up on the meals they missed because of the inclement weather.

Perhaps the greatest benefit of hunting pre-rut whitetails is being able to hunt in mild weather. There is nothing more enjoyable than hunting whitetails when the weather is comfortable. True, deer might not move as much as when cold weather arrives, but it's a special experience to be in a treestand as the last rays of sunlight fade from the forest. So, don't wait for the rut because if you do you may find you were late to the party.

CHAPTER 8

Timing the Rut

Nothing intrigues or motivates America's whitetail hunters quite like the rut. Simply put, it is the straw that stirs the deer hunter's drink. The memories of past whitetail ruts form the basis for future possibilities and keep hunters going back to the whitetail woods year after year.

The whitetail's rut is an amazing and complex phenomenon. It's made up of an array of behavioral traits, each distinctly different but interwoven. In Chapter 9 I'll share how I hunt the various phases of the rut. This chapter will set the stage for these chapters by discussing a fascinating rut-related research project I've been involved with for over a decade.

▶ Genesis of the Work

After practically living with nature for over half a century, I'm still in awe of the way God pieced our universe together. What a creator! Everything He created is precise and perfect. Each natural phenomenon has a reason for existing. It's truly amazing how the natural world influences every aspect of the whitetail's life.

Bucks often display aggressive chasing behavior when pursuing a doe. Such chases often last for up to half an hour or more.

For the last 12 years, Vermont wildlife biologist Wayne Laroche and I have been researching the influence the sun and moon have on the timing of the whitetail rut in the North, specifically north of the 35th latitude. In its twelfth year, the project is expected to run for fifteen years before being completed. Why so long? There are a number of reasons, but the primary factor is the fluctuation in the timing of what I refer to as the whitetail's rutting moon, which is the second full moon after the autumnal equinox.

Native Americans had the whitetail's rut figured out long before the Europeans arrived. By way of example, the Dakota Sioux Indian tribe called the November full moon (the eleventh full moon of the year) "Moon when antlers are broken off, Moon when deer copulate." Interesting! Granted, they had centuries to figure out the whitetail rut but nonetheless they had it down to a science and knew that the November full moon would be the trigger that set the whitetail rut in motion.

Those who have followed our work know that the timing of the rutting moon comes within a day or

two of repeating itself every 11 years and reasonably close to repeating itself every three to four years. Consequently, it's important to collect good data over an extended period of time in order to evaluate the moon's impact on white-tailed deer rutting activity.

Though we've been collecting data for the last twelve years, our interest in this project was born nearly two decades ago.

Laroche is a respected biologist and the current Commissioner of Fish and Wildlife for the state of Vermont. He is also an avid whitetail hunter who often spends the entire month of November in Vermont and northern Maine chasing big woods bucks.

He became interested in the moon's influence on whitetails after researching the impact the moon has on grouper fish in the Caribbean and the Gulf of Mexico. As he hunted Vermont and Maine woods every year, he noticed distinct fluctuations in whitetail activity patterns. After studying the yearly changes he began to wonder if the moon was affecting the way whitetails behaved during November, just as it had

When the second full moon after the autumnal equinox arrives in the north, the stage is set for the rut to become full blown.

Motion sensing cameras are used to collect data on deer activity during the autumn months. They are placed along well-used trails, between bedding and feeding areas.

influenced the fish he had studied over the years.

My interest in lunar-related behavior began in the mid-1980s while hunting and photographing. Up until then I had bought into the research data that originated in the 1950s and '60s that said the peak breeding period for whitetails in my region of the North (42nd latitude) would be November 15 to 20 each year.

Over a 10-year period (1985 to 1995) I had the opportunity to photograph whitetails extensively on a large property in the Adirondack Mountains of New York. During this time I shot hundreds of rolls of film and kept detailed notes on deer behavior. Despite the deer population and the adult-doe-to-antlered-buck ratio remaining constant, the peak breeding period was seldom the same from year to year. Some years the breeding took place in early November, some years mid-November, and a few years late November. It was obvious to me that something more than photoperiod, or shortening day length, was driving the timing of the rut's seeking, chasing and breeding phases.

In the early 1990s I became aware of work Laroche was doing that dealt with the relationship between the width of a whitetail's hoof and its body size. To learn more, I interviewed him for a magazine article I was writing. We shared many things about ourselves and our love for whitetail hunting. During the course of our discussion we talked about the variations we were seeing in the timing of whitetail rutting behavior. I'll never forget Wayne's comment that he believed the moon was responsible for the fluctuations in deer activity that we were observing during November.

After our conversation, we decided to see if the moon had anything to do with the timing of the whitetail rut.

▶The Theory

As further background, here is the theory for our research. At some point in autumn, the amount of daylight decreases enough to reset the whitetail's reproductive clock, thus placing the breeding season in November, December and January in the Northern Hemisphere. Once the doe's reproductive cycle is reset by a specific amount of daylight, her estrus cycle is ready to be cued by moonlight, which provides a bright light stimulus to the pineal gland several nights in a row each lunar month. Then, the rapid decrease in lunar brightness during the moon's third quarter triggers hormonal production by the pineal gland. Physiological changes prompted by the pineal gland culminate in ovulation and estrus.

A northern doe's estrogen level peaks around November 1, as does a buck's sperm count. With both sexes poised to breed, it stands to reason a mechanism must be in place if the doe is to enter estrus and be bred under the darker phases of the moon, which are the third through the first quarters. *That mechanism in the North (north of about*

During the rut several bucks will work the same scrape, especially if the scrape is in a prime travel corridor.

This chart illustrates when the rut's seeking, chasing and breeding phases blend into each other in relation to the rutting moon, which is by definition the second full moon after the autumnal equinox.

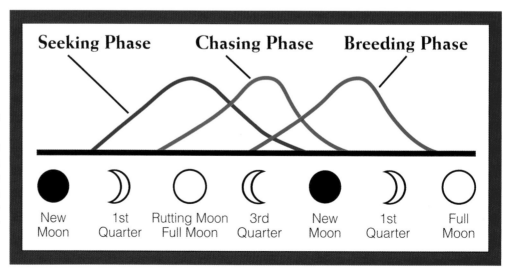

Seeking Phase   Chasing Phase   Breeding Phase

New Moon | 1st Quarter | Rutting Moon Full Moon | 3rd Quarter | New Moon | 1st Quarter | Full Moon

When the rut ramps up a buck will lip-curl whenever it finds a place a doe has urinated.

the 35ᵗʰ latitude) is the second full moon after the autumnal equinox, which we call the rutting moon.

▶ The Research

With each passing year, we've added more and more data collection devices to the research project. In the beginning, we monitored just six does. Now, we are collecting data for our research from up to 100 does.

We also monitor air temperature, weather patterns and moonlight intensity throughout the fall. In addition, we use twelve motion-sensing timers to record deer activity throughout each day. Four of the timers are in my farm's 35-acre high-fenced whitetail research facility and up to eight are positioned in other areas of our farm and surrounding properties to monitor the wild, free-ranging deer population. The data, which is collected from October through December, is

downloaded to our computers for analysis.

Unlike twelve years ago, when no one was helping us, we now have several serious deer hunters and outfitters across North America who are in the woods every day during the fall keeping detailed journals to chronicle deer behavior in their region of the country. This added information has allowed us to better understand what is happening in other parts of North America during October, November and December.

With well over 15,000 data points of information in our system, we've concluded that the second full moon after the autumnal equinox (the time each fall when there are 12 hours of daylight and 12 hours of darkness) stimulates both buck and doe rutting activity. Based on past data, we know that when the rutting moon falls anywhere from late October to November 12, the timing of the seeking, chasing and breeding phases of the rut is very predictable; we refer to this as a "classic rut."

During the years when the rutting moon appears later (like 1997, 2002 and 2005 when it occurred on November 14, 19 and 16 respectively in the North), we've discovered that the timing of the rut's seeking, chasing and breeding phases is just a little different. When the rutting moon arrives on or after November 14, we've found that the rut progresses more rapidly than when the rutting moon arrives in late October or early in November.

Basically, the data is showing that when the rutting moon arrives late, the seeking begins three or four days before the full moon, just as we've always predicted. However, we've discovered that once the full moon occurs, the chasing is frenzied and the prime breeding kicks in within a day or two of the full moon's appearance rather than a week after its arrival, as it does in years when the rutting moon appears in early November. Two years in our research project that illustrate this well are 1997, when the rutting moon was November 14, and 2002, when it arrived on November 19.

In 1997 the data showed that the seeking and chasing phases of the rut didn't happen until November 12 to 21. Breeding kicked in within a couple days after the rutting moon and ran through the end of the month.

The 2002 findings are nearly identical to 1997. In 2002, all but one reporting location indicated seeking and chasing peaked between November 16 and 22 in the North. Breeding began around November 19 and 20 and peaked Thanksgiving week (November 24 to 28). There also was a fair amount of breeding still occurring the first few days of December.

▶ Rut Suppressors

To varying degrees the project has revealed several factors that can affect the amount of deer activity observed during daylight hours. As was outlined in Chapter 5, the suppressing effects of severe storms, warm air temperature, poor adult-doe-to-antlered-buck ratios, changing food sources and human pressure can have a detrimental effect on day time deer activity.

Any one of these suppressors can keep deer from moving on their own. However, when one or more are coupled together strange things can occur to change the rut's complexion.

▶ The Maine Lab

In order to get a better read on the moon's influence on whitetail rutting behavior, Laroche and I have started to look more closely at how deer move in areas where humans, poor adult doe-to-antlered buck ratios, warm temperatures, and baiting have

Ten years of research has shown that deer activity begins increasing when the second full moon after the autumnal equinox arrives and peaks a couple of days after the third quarter. Breeding data has shown that the majority of breeding occurs from the third to first quarter that follows the rutting mood.

Rubs of this size are often worked by multiple mature bucks.

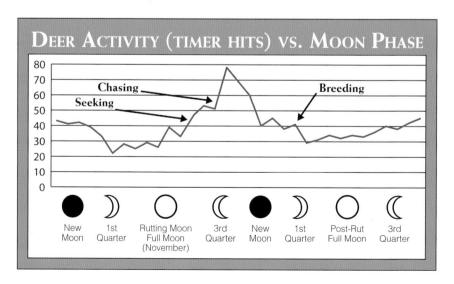

DEER ACTIVITY (TIMER HITS) VS. MOON PHASE

Chasing
Seeking
Breeding

New Moon | 1st Quarter | Rutting Moon Full Moon (November) | 3rd Quarter | New Moon | 1st Quarter | Post-Rut Full Moon | 3rd Quarter

Big woods deer trackers, like Dick Bernier of Maine, have greatly helped the research project because of their insights into rutting behavior.

During the chase phase of the rut, chasing behavior often creates exciting encounters for hunters.

a minimal impact. There are few places in the United States where such conditions exist, but northern Maine is one of them.

The whitetails found in this region are not pressured by man. Nature (i.e., deep snows and predators) keeps the adult doe-to-antlered buck ratio at less than three to one, baiting is not allowed, and warm temperatures are not as common as they are in other regions of the country. What makes Maine so unique is that it has mature bucks in the population and snow is often present to tip off serious trackers as to what is going on in the deer world. So, with few rut suppressors present, the far northern portion of this vacationland is the ultimate place to study the moon's effect on deer activity.

As mentioned earlier, Laroche often spends the entire month of November in a northern Maine deer camp, living out of an 18´x52´ wall tent. His camp is limited to eight hunters at a time and each night Laroche debriefs every hunter, asking them to recall the number of scrapes and rubs observed, the number of deer sightings by sex, the types of behavior witnessed, and any other species of animals that were seen. This data is then analyzed and incorporated into our database. Laroche and his party cover a remote area of fifty to one hundred square miles on any given day.

Dick Bernier is *Deer and Deer Hunting* magazine's Northeast field editor and a hunting legend in the state of Maine. He has written two popular books on tracking white-tailed deer, and like Laroche, he spends the entire month of November in the northern Maine bush tracking the biggest bucks he can find.

Interestingly, Bernier and his hunting party realized long ago that there was a correlation between November's full moon and the timing of the whitetail's rut. When I began writing about the moon's impact on the rut, Bernier contacted me to let me know that they concurred with the findings of our research. They also offered us access to their records.

At the end of each day, Bernier and his companions log into their journals everything they observe and after the season forward their information to Laroche and me. As one might expect, the observations of Laroche's and Bernier's parties are near mirrors of each other.

▶The Yearling Factor

Throughout the research we've heard from hunters who have stated that they have seen chasing going on at different times than we have predicted. What's going on? In over 95% of the cases our follow up has revealed that these sightings were of yearling bucks chasing does.

Yearling behavior during the rut can be very misleading. I've raised many yearlings and witnessed enough wild-free-ranging yearling behavior to tell you that they are almost 100% out of phase with mature buck behavior during the rut.

The bottom line to yearling buck behavior is that

NORTH & SOUTH DIVIDING LINE FOR RUTTING DATES

35TH LATITUDE

When the majority of a region's buck population is made up of yearlings, it is difficult to see the rut unfold in the same way as when mature bucks dominate a population.

they are constantly on the move throughout the fall (when temps are normal or cooler) and chase about every doe they encounter, from September on. Consequently, the frenzied, immature behavior typically exhibited by yearling bucks has a tendency to throw deer hunters a curve when it comes to understanding what is really taking place regarding the rut

▶ Don't Be Fooled

In the North, a whitetail buck's testosterone level peaks around November 1 each year. When this happens bucks are so "juiced" they can hardly contain themselves. Consequently they will begin cruising and at times chase does, leaving the hunter with the impression that the rut has begun. In reality this is usually not the case.

In years when the rutting moon falls during the first few days of November, a buck's testosterone peak and a doe's estrous cycle synchronize at approximately the same time, causing all elements of the rut to come together at the same time. When the rutting moon falls around November 10 or later, things will be different. In such years there will be a flurry of buck activity around November 1, followed by a crash in activity for about a week prior to the rutting moon. Once the rutting moon arrives, the rut ramps up and chaos comes to the deer woods. This phenomenon can be seen in the sidebar on page 84, "Deer Activity (Timer Hits) vs. Moon Phase."

▶ What About the South?

Since 1995, there has been much discussion about how accurate our lunar project is when it comes to timing the whitetail's rut in areas south of the 35th latitude (Alabama, Arkansas, Georgia, Tennessee, Florida, Mississippi, South Carolina, Texas, etc.).

Southern whitetails don't face the harsh winters and brutal conditions that dictate when Northern white-tailed fawns must be born to ensure they are large enough to survive severe winters. Harsh cold and deep snows aren't part of the Southern equation, so weather isn't as great a factor for fawn births. Therefore, the South's rut appears to be driven by less obvious factors, such as climate, genetics, nutrition, doe-to-buck ratios, day-length and moon phases.

States like Florida, Alabama, Louisiana and Texas have multiple rutting dates. However, after years of collecting observational data from Southern sources, Wayne Laroche and I are very confident that deer in these locales are cued by the full moon. The trick is determining whether it is the October, November or December full moon.

Texas is a good example. I've hunted the south Texas brush country many times, and it's obvious its rut begins on the third full moon after the autumnal equinox (rutting moon). It's crucial to check with a local biologist to find out what month the rut typically occurs in a specific location. You can then pinpoint the full moon that occurs during that time. This full moon is your rutting moon.

▶ Synopsis

Enlightening is one of the best words I know of to describe this research project. It amazes me that the relationship between the moon and the timing of the rut was not discovered long ago. We set out to run the project for fifteen years, and although we could probably wrap it up now because of the repeatable patterns we've observed and documented, we fully expect to stay the course. Our fascination with the project keeps our interest level high.

As a quick recap, keep in mind that the seeking, chasing and breeding phases of the northern whitetail rut will occur as follows:

When the second full moon after the autumnal equinox falls between late October and November 12, the seeking phase of the rut will start approximately three to four days before the full moon and run three to four days after it. The chasing phase will kick in a couple days after the full moon and be intense for about ten days following the full moon. The breeding phase will begin about seven days after the full moon and last about fourteen days thereafter if the herd is fine-tuned (meaning it has good nutrition, good habitat, a good sex ratio, and a well represented mature buck population). Note that the phases will overlap somewhat.

When the second full moon after the autumnal equinox occurs on November 14 or later, the seeking phase will begin approximately three days before the full moon. The chasing phase will begin a little earlier than normal, and the breeding phase will occur from the full moon to fourteen days thereafter in fine-tuned herds. So, when the rutting moon appears late, the breeding phase takes place a little sooner than when it appears in early November.

▶ The Rut's Sweet Spot

Not everyone has the flexibility to block out the whole month of November in order to have a ringside seat to the whitetail rut. The benefit of this research is to let hunters and deer lovers know the optimal times to hunt and observe the whitetail rut.

It's important to remember that the whitetail's rut is not a 100-yard dash to the finish line. To put it in human

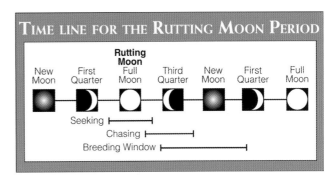

TIME LINE FOR THE RUTTING MOON PERIOD

New Moon — First Quarter — **Rutting Moon** Full Moon — Third Quarter — New Moon — First Quarter — Full Moon

Seeking
Chasing
Breeding Window

Predicting the Future: 2005 to 2020

Year	Rutting Moon	Prime Seek-Chase phase	Prime Breeding Window
2005	Nov. 16	Nov. 12-22	Nov. 19-Dec. 3
2006	Nov. 6	Nov. 3-13	Nov. 12-26
2007	Oct. 25	Oct. 23-Nov. 3	Nov. 1-14
2008	Nov. 12	Nov. 9-19	Nov. 18-Dec. 2
2009	Nov. 2	Oct. 31-Nov. 10	Nov. 9-23
2010	Nov. 20	Nov. 16-27	Nov. 22-Dec. 6
2011	Nov. 10	Nov. 7-18	Nov. 16-30
2012	Oct. 29	Oct. 26-Nov. 7	Nov. 6-20
2013	Nov. 17	Nov. 13-23	Nov. 19-Dec. 3
2014	Nov. 7	Nov. 4-14	Nov. 13-27
2015	Oct. 27	Oct. 24-Nov. 6	Nov. 4-18
2016	Nov. 14	Nov. 10-21	Nov. 17-Dec. 1
2017	Nov. 3	Nov. 1-10	Nov. 10-24
2018	Oct. 24	Oct. 21-Nov. 1	Oct. 31-Nov. 13
2019	Nov. 11	Nov. 8-19	Nov. 17-Dec.1
2020	Oct. 31	Oct. 28-Nov. 9	Nov. 7-21

These dates are for the north.

terms it's more like a marathon where the contestants run along at a brisk pace for 26+ miles. In a fine-tuned deer herd the rut's length will be approximately 40 days long.

However, there is a sweet spot in the rut – a time when rutting behavior is at maximum force. All things being equal the rut's sweet spot will begin about three days after the rutting moon and last for about ten days. During this time bucks are frantically rubbing, scraping, fighting, scouring their territory and chasing nearly every doe they encounter. This is the golden time for a hunter to be in the woods.

Once the full-blown breeding begins deer activity grinds to a much slower pace because now the rut's tempo is dictated by doe movement during the breeding phase. This is why the breeding phase of the rut is more difficult to hunt than the seeking and chasing phase that precedes it.

CHAPTER 9

Hunting the Rut

Although whitetail bucks scrape, rub and chase does, it's the does that create the rut. Therefore, my hunting strategy revolves around pursuing mature white-tailed bucks as they react and interact with doe groups.

As previously mentioned, a whitetail's rutting switch is usually thrown by late October (in the North). For the next 30 to 40 days, a buck develops an ever-increasing case of "sexitis." During this time, bucks let their guard down and become vulnerable. Once the rut's breeding phase is full-blown, a buck becomes harder to hunt because he's around does. So the best window of opportunity for hunting the rutting moon, which is the second full moon after the fall equinox, is about three or four days before the full moon until about seven to ten days afterwards.

A whitetail's range can be broken into three zones: feeding, bedding and the area in between, which I call the transition zone. If pressure isn't severe, the transition zone is where I ambush the most bucks during the rut. There are five reasons for this:

1. Mature bucks seldom frequent prime feeding areas during daylight hours.

2. If they do, does are usually nearby and the scene can resemble a fire drill when the chasing begins.

3. With several deer in the feeding area, you have all kinds of eyes to contend with before the moment of truth arrives.

4. You must stay out of the bedding area to keep a mature buck from changing its habits.

5. The transition zone is where most rutting sign will be found and where a buck is most vulnerable.

▶Transition Zones

Most of the time I hunt transition zones during the rutting moon period to kill a mature buck. To build upon what I wrote about scrapes previously, the following relates to transition zones and scrapes.

Generally, a transition zone is anywhere from 50 yards to over a mile in length. It all depends on how far the bedding area is from the feeding area, or how far one bedding area is from another. If a transition zone is thick, has predictable winds, or happens to be a natural funnel, your chances for success increase.

If conditions and habitat are right, a number of trails will pass through a transition zone. It's along and near these trails that I look for key rutting sign in mid-October. As with pre-rut scouting, I go into these areas between mid-morning and noon as inconspicuously as possible while searching for sign. For the most part, I don't have to spend a lot of time in any one location because my off-season scouting has shown me where to look.

Nearly every good licking branch gets worked in a buck's core area during the rut's seeking and chasing phase. Once breeding becomes prevalent, scraping behavior begins to decrease.

▶Scrapes – Whitetail Stop Signs

As the rutting moon arrives and the rut intensifies, three distinct types of scrapes show up: boundary, random and primary.

Boundary scrapes: Boundary scrapes are made randomly as bucks travel through their territory. These

THE BEST TIMES TO HUNT

Deer Movement by Hour of Day

(Line graph: y-axis labeled "# Movements per Day" from 0 to 80; x-axis labeled "Hour of Day" from 0 to 22.)

Not all scrapes are prime scrapes. I only hunt those that are in prime travel corridors.

scrapes often show up along the edges of fields, fencerows and old roadways. Those made along field edges are nearly always made at night. Because of this I pay little attention to these scrapes except for checking the track sizes. If the track is more than 2-1/4 inches wide (with no more than a 1/4-inch split in the toes) the buck probably is over 2-1/2 years old and nearing maturity. Such bucks also will tip the scales at over 175 pounds in the North.

Random scrapes: Random scrapes are just that – scrapes that are made spontaneously as a buck cruises his territory. A buck will often make a random scrape whenever he comes upon an attractive licking branch and is "moved" to work the site. Seldom will they be reused and in most cases are not serious candidates for a hunting set up.

Primary scrapes: Primary scrapes are the ones hunters need to pay attention to. In many ways they are the "mother lode" of whitetail scrapes, with some having the potential of becoming the true "bus station" for whitetail bucks. They are normally found in strategic locations, inside corners, ridge lines and especially along well worn trails between bedding and feeding areas during the rut. In many instances bucks will make a line of scrapes (20 to 50 yards apart) along such trails. Because many primary scrapes are found along well-worn trails, more than one buck will work and rework them during the three phases of the rut. I've made a career of hunting and killing bucks along well-used trails. I've probably killed more bucks over primary scrapes along well-used runways than any other place.

▶ Scrape Hunting Strategy

I try to plan my scrape hunting around three or four good scrape locations, rotating between them so as not to over-hunt any one.

I killed this 140-class P&Y buck 10 days after the rutting moon in 2001, while he worked one of my mock licking branches. What made this harvest fulfilling was that I had passed up this buck 5 times the previous year when it was a 110" 2-1/2 year-old buck.

When I find a traditional signpost rub like this one I get excited. Such rubs are used year after year, providing the buck's rubbing does not kill the tree.

Because I'll be rattling and calling from these ambush points, I look for hot scrapes surrounded by medium to heavy cover. If I find a highly used area that looks good for an ambush I take steps to enhance the location by making sure the scrape has a great licking branch above it. My goal is to make it so attractive that no deer (buck or doe) can resist stopping to work it when it passes through the area.

I used to enhance all scrapes I hunted over with liberal amounts of lure. Though I will occasionally doctor a scrape with 100% fresh whitetail urine I've discovered that I can waive this process by letting deer do their own doctoring. When a site is active every buck that works the scrape will urinate there, providing far more scent than I could ever hope to provide.

Whenever I approach a scrape to check it or doctor it, I do so as scent-free as possible. To accomplish this I wear rubber boots and latex gloves when near or working on a scrape location. This precaution is a must.

▶ Rubs & Rub Lines— Whitetail Billboards

Often, where you find scraping you'll find rubbing. They go hand in glove, so when you find heavy rubbing in an area of heavy scraping your chances of success increase greatly. I always look for traditional signpost rubs wherever I hunt. Such rubs are normally made on trees 6+ inches thick and rubbed year after year. Unfortunately it takes a good population of mature bucks for a true traditional signpost rub to exist, so, in most of the whitetail's range, where 75+ percent of the buck kill is yearlings, there are no signpost rubs.

If a signpost rub cannot be found, look for big rubs, rub lines and clusters of rubs in the transition zone. Rub lines often reveal the way a buck was traveling. If the scarred side of the tree faces the feeding area, the rub was probably made in the morning as the buck returned to his bedding area. If the scar faces the bedding area, the rub or rubs were undoubtedly made when the buck exited in the evening.

If there is a definite line of big rubs in an area, a stand should be hung downwind of it. Such a rub line is a visual aid showing the area where a buck likes to travel.

One piece of rubbing sign that gets my attention in a scraping area is a cluster of rubs. When you find a cluster of rubs in a prime scraping area or an active funnel, you know there are a lot of bucks around. And if there is a good population of does, there's even more reason to be excited. It is believed that heavy rubbing by bucks leaves pheromones that help induce does to come into estrus.

It takes a big, mature buck to make a rub like this. As the rut progresses, rubs like this will become more common if there are mature bucks in the area.

This is a great rub line. If you find a line of rubs like this one immediately try to hunt the area.

▶ Talk the Language

Whitetails are no different from other animals in that they are curious creatures. Throughout their lives they communicate with each other using a variety of bleats, grunts snorts and wheezes. For the first six months of life, fawns bleat and mew to their mothers. Adult bucks and does also communicate with each other by grunting and bleating. Whitetail bucks wheeze and snort to show aggression and both sexes commonly snort to alert other deer of danger. During the rutting moon, when the rut is ramping up, bucks also respond to the sound of two bucks fighting. Using antlers, grunt tubes and other calls to communicate with whitetails during autumn months can be challenging, exciting and on occasion, very productive.

▶ Calling

Calling has revolutionized the way I hunt whitetails and increased my success immensely.

When I began calling deer, I only used antlers. Though there were successes, it wasn't until I began using a grunt tube, alone and in conjunction with antlers, that my success at luring deer close increased significantly. During the last 20 years, I've discovered that deer are more responsive to a call than anything else. For this reason my grunt tube goes with me whether I'm hunting with gun, bow or camera. Regardless of where I hunt in North America, I find that for every buck I rattle in, up to 20 will respond to grunting, bleating and wheezing.

Whether you are a novice or seasoned veteran, it's important to realize that you don't need to know how to make every vocalization a whitetail is able to make. Researchers have isolated between 200 and

During the seeking and chasing phase of the rut fighting can be frequent and spectacular.

This is the end result of one of the most exciting hunts I've ever had on our farm. Five days after the rutting moon I rattled and called this buck to my stand. I shot him immediately after he worked one of my mock scrapes.

400 different sounds deer make (depending on which research you look at). You do not have to know them all. There are four basic sounds (with variations) that whitetails make: bleat, grunt, wheeze and snort. Master these and you will be amazed by how many bucks you can call within shooting range.

My favorite calls are the bleat, fawn bleat, basic grunt, trailing grunt, tending grunt, wheeze and aggressive-snort.

Bleat: I find the bleat to be a good locator/coaxing call, much like a turkey yelp. I often use the bleat a couple of times just before and after I do a rattling sequence. I'll also use it when the action is slow and I haven't seen a deer in a while. Basically it sounds like *neeeeaaah*. A bleat is easy to learn on most grunt tubes and a no-brainer if you have one of the popular gravity bleat canisters that are very popular. These canisters have holes in the top of them and when tipped upside down make a whitetail bleat.

Fawn bleat: The fawn bleat is very similar to the bleat but the major difference is that it is high pitched, like you would expect for a young animal. The fawn bleat is a phenomenal call for photographers who hunt whitetails throughout the year and for late season deer hunters. I've called countless does and bucks within camera range during the summer months using this call. During this time of the year nearly all adult deer will be on high alert when they respond. When used during the autumn months the fawn bleat is an excellent locator call. Bucks that hear it will often come to check it out

because they know there must be a doe in the area.

Basic Grunt: Grunting is the vocalization of choice for whitetails. Bucks, does and fawns grunt. When it comes to the grunting sound that deer make it should be noted that all grunts do not sound the same because of each deer's physical difference. No two deer will sound exactly the same. I've learned this through in-the-field experience and nearly fifteen years of raising deer. By way of example, I can be in my deer enclosure, out of sight of a deer that is grunting, and often know which buck is grunting.

The tone of the grunt will often depend on the maturity level of the buck. Older bucks have a lot of bass to their voice, meaning their grunts sound very guttural. For the most part I will not use a deep-throated guttural grunt unless I know I'm communicating with a mature buck. If you try using such a grunt on a yearling or 2-1/2 year old buck there is the distinct possibility that he'll turn tail and flee.

Most of the grunt tubes on the market are capable of accurately making both doe and guttural buck grunts. Both are easy to make. Unless I can identify the buck's size, or know from the grunting sound that it's a mature buck, I'll give off one to four medium-tone grunts.

If I'm on stand and hear a buck grunt, but can't see him, I'll immediately grunt back. If the buck is not with a doe he'll usually come looking for the deer that made the sound. The key is to never be tentative when a buck grunts first.

Trailing grunt: The trailing grunt is a short grunt

of other bucks. There are times that a buck will grunt or snort before wheezing but more often than not will wheeze only. I make the wheeze naturally by inhaling over my tongue, with my cheeks tight to the edge of my tongue. It can be hard to master naturally and I suggest that you purchase a good behavioral video that illustrates the vocalizations in order to learn the sounds whitetails make. There are also a number of commercial calls on the market that can make the wheeze.

Aggressive-snort: The aggressive-snort will put whitetails on high alert. In spite of this there are times to consider using it. When breeding parties form (when more than one buck is trying to breed the same doe) aggressive snorting often takes place by bucks attempting to intimidate each other. Often when I'm doing a rattling sequence I'll make two to three snorts while I'm clashing the antlers together. This is not a call you will want to use often but during the chase and breeding phases of the rut it can be worth your time to use it while rattling. Use sparingly and with caution.

▶ What to Expect

As with spring turkey hunting, you never know what to expect from a whitetail buck when you call at him. Every whitetail is different. Some bucks have little desire to mix it up socially with other deer. Consequently, they are nearly impossible to call within range. Others respond very well. So, you never know what you'll get, but unless you try you will never know what could be.

If a whitetail buck is with a doe, especially an estrus doe, he will be very hard (if not impossible) to call within range. The wheeze, or a soft snort followed immediately by a loud wheeze is about the only way I've succeeded in doing so. A buck that leaves an estrous doe for this aggressive tactic will be looking for a fight when he comes to the sound.

▶ Rattling

During the rutting moon, bucks are very aggressive. Often, all it takes for a fight to occur is for one buck to look at another buck the wrong way. Over the years I've found that the best time to use antlers to bring a buck close to my stand is from about a week before the rutting

Never climb into a stand during the rut without a deer call. Next to your weapon, it's the most important piece of equipment you have.

that bucks make when traveling through the woods or when around other deer. It's not uncommon for a rut-crazed buck to make a short grunt every one to 10 steps if he's in the right mood. If I see a buck walking through the woods, I'll use this grunt to stop him and to coax him in my direction. This is also a call that I use when no deer are in sight. If a buck is sexually active but not with a doe, there is a good chance he'll respond to a grunt.

Tending grunt: The tending grunt can be a lethal weapon if used properly. When a buck is with a hot doe and is either frustrated by her rejections or is interrupted by another buck, he'll make a grunt that has a ticking cadence. If I'm hunting in thick cover during the rut and a buck walks within sight of the stand, I'll use a tending grunt to bring him within range. This is a great call to use when bucks are on the move and the rut is boiling over.

Wheeze: The wheeze is an aggressive sound that bucks make when they are irritated by the presence

When using a buck decoy have the antlered decoy positioned 20 to 25 yards in front of the stand facing you.

moon to the third phase of the moon, which is seven days after the full moon. The seven days that follow the rutting moon have proven to be my best rattling period.

When I rattle during the rut I do so aggressively, with a sequence that seldom lasts longer than 2 or 3 minutes. Few fights I've witnessed during the rut have ever lasted longer, so I keep it short and loud and make it as aggressive sounding as possible. Generally, I rattle for a minute, pause for about 30 seconds, and rattle again for a minute or two. Don't over-rattle; rather, space the rattling sequences about 40 minutes apart. I've also found that rattling during the two-hour period either side of darkness works best. However, don't rule out midday. I've rattled in some nice bucks when the rutting moon was full and the hourglass said 12 o'clock. A few years ago I killed a great 160-class buck shortly after completing a rattling sequence at 12:15 p.m.

When rattling, try to do it in the thickest cover possible, especially if you're bow hunting. When a buck responds to antlers he will come in cautiously, looking for the combatants. If he can't see them, he'll usually hang up. Thick cover forces him to come closer. Though you can't make as many natural sounds, like breaking branches and raking the ground when perched in a tree, rattling from a tree stand gives greater concealment and allows you to see the buck coming.

When rattling I use real 130-class antlers that have no weather checks in them. The fresher the antlers are the better they will sound. The problem with antlers smaller than this is that they are difficult to hear from a distance. If antlers are 140+ B&C they shouldn't be in

your hands, they should be on the wall.

The success rate for rattling will depend on the quality of the deer herd where you are hunting. If the herd is fine-tuned, meaning the adult-doe-to-antlered-buck-ratio is not greater than 2 to 1 and there are mature bucks in the population, rattling will work well. If the area's sex ratio is skewed heavily toward does with mostly yearling bucks, rattling will seldom work.

▶ Decoying

In 1989 I was one of the first hunters/photographers to seriously use whitetail decoys to lure whitetails within range. Since then, I've hunted and photographed over decoys from New York to Texas to Saskatchewan. In the beginning I thought, "This is too easy." I quickly learned that there were many do's and don'ts in using decoys. Decoys will work to bring in deer throughout the fall but I've found the seeking phase through the breeding period, to be the best time for decoys, be it buck or doe.

Because incoming whitetail bucks almost always circle the decoy, I prefer 3-D units over silhouettes. As good as today's decoys appear to be, their most common shortcoming is lack of motion. Without some kind of motion, decoys, at best, work only about half the time. From my earliest days of decoying I realized that to be successful I needed to make approaching bucks more curious and less cautious about the decoy I was using for bow hunting.

Though it took a little effort, I remedied the situation by attaching a paper clamp (sold at office supply stores) to the rump of the decoy. I use the clamp to hold a white handkerchief, and I tie monofilament fishing line to the handkerchief and run the line to my tree stand. Then, after attaching the line to my boot I'm able to add just enough tail flickering to the decoy for a buck to think the decoy is real.

Deer do not always pick up a decoy's presence easily if the decoy is in thick cover. So for best results, decoys should be placed at the edge of a field or in a well traveled funnel where deer can easily see them.

Because 3-D decoys can be cumbersome and noisy to assemble, think through the process of how you're going to get them to your hunting position. If you

Position a doe decoy 15 to 20 yards from the stand facing away from you.

Our research has revealed that the first three hours of the day is the best time to be on stand.

must assemble them every time you use them, do the assembly at least 100 yards from where you intend to hunt. Nothing will ruin a set-up quicker than plastic parts banging together. Also, never leave a decoy set up when you are not hunting over it. Once a deer has been fooled by a decoy, your chances of fooling it again are almost zero. If you must leave the decoy in your hunting area make sure it is covered with pine bows or other natural vegetation.

Three things are very important when readying a decoy for hunting:

1. Rid the decoy of any human odor by spraying it liberally with scent eliminator.

2. Make sure the decoy is anchored to the ground. The last thing you want is for it to fall over in the wind or from the soft touch of a deer.

3. Never carry a decoy without wearing blaze orange. Today's decoys are authentic looking and for this reason safety is paramount when moving them around.

Doe decoy: When bow hunting with a doe decoy, try to place it 15 to 20 yards upwind of your stand, with the decoy facing or quartering away from you. In most cases, a buck will circle a doe decoy, rather than coming straight to it. Also, if a buck suspects something is odd about the scene it will hang up within 20 to 30 yards from the decoy. Normally, within seconds it begins stomping or snorting, then

flees. By placing the doe decoy at least 15 yards from your stand, you will be able to get a shot when the buck hangs up. This will often be at point blank range. If a buck comes all the way to the decoy it will usually give you a broadside or quartering away shot while it explores the backside of the doe decoy.

Buck decoy: When bow hunting with a buck decoy, the strategy should be a little different. I place the buck decoy about 20 yards upwind of my stand with it facing or quartering toward me. Unlike the doe decoy, where the buck approaches from the rear, a buck will usually approach a buck decoy from the front. So, it's best to have the buck decoy facing you. The antlers I use on the decoy are always representative of the area I'm hunting. In high-pressure areas where there are few mature bucks this means nothing larger than 100-class Boone and Crocket antlers. Always remember that bucks size each other up by body, antler size or a combination of both. This sets the tone for their aggression toward each other. Using only one antler or having the decoy's ears pulled back will suggest that the decoy is a fighter, thus stimulating aggression.

If you bow hunt over a buck decoy and the approaching buck is one you want to harvest (and shows an aggressive attitude) you'll need to shoot before he reaches the decoy. If you wait for him to get to the decoy, the speed of the resulting frenzied fight will make a shot impossible.

CHAPTER 10

Hunting the Post-Rut

In most of North America, hunting during December's post-rut is a far cry from the helter-skelter action that takes place during the previous month's rut. The difference between November's rut and December's post-rut can often be as different as night and day. There are a few reasons for this. A whitetail's biological make-up at this time of the year and the amount of human pressure it has encountered from September to December help explain why post-rut bucks can be the hardest of all whitetails to hunt.

The rut research that Wayne Laroche and I are doing leads us to believe that in a fine-tuned deer herd about 70% to 80% of mature does breed during the rutting moon period. Our findings show that only 10% to 15% of the North's doe population gets bred in December. So, with the majority of the North's doe population already bred by December, the picture can look rather bleak for a hunter expecting any semblance of November's rut.

By the time a buck makes it through November's breeding ordeal and inches into December he's a far cry from the muscular rutting machine he was when the rutting moon hung high in the sky. A white-tailed buck in the post-rut is typically 20% to 25%

Because Hunting pressure is normally low during the post-rut, tracking a buck can be a productive way to hunt and kill a trophy.

Still-hunting can be a very productive way of hunting post-rut bucks. The strategy should be to move into the wind (or with a crosswind), at a snail's pace, with your eyes scanning the woods.

lighter in weight than when he entered November. It's not uncommon to see mature whitetail bucks at this time of the year on the verge of physical meltdown. By the time the post-rut moon hangs in the sky, a buck's priorities have changed from sex to survival, in spite of the fact that 10% to 15% of the does are yet to be bred.

▶ Post-Rut Biology

There is no doubt that many hunters question a buck's decreased desire to breed in December in the North, especially when magazines tout the virtues of the so-called "second rut." A buck's ability to keep up

the rutting chase in the post-rut moon is possible, but in most cases highly unlikely. Why? Research (Lambase 1972) shows that a buck's sperm count in December is about half what it was in November. So, physically, the drive isn't there. As a result, bucks are calmer, more collected animals when the post-rut moon arrives.

Because survival is now his main objective, a buck becomes a different creature in December and early January. Oh, he will still breed, and often does, but generally he isn't out looking for does the way he was in October and November. Rather, he feeds, rests and takes what comes his way.

Be prepared to see chasing and breeding take place during the post-rut because 10% to 15% of the doe population will breed during this time.

When December arrives in the North, the entire deer family group gravitates toward known food sources, such as cornfields in farm country or cedar swamp yarding areas in wilderness regions. The main objective of bucks and does during this time is food, food, food. As a result, trying to hunt rub and scrape lines as you did in October and November is, for the most part, a waste of time.

▶ Man's Influence on the Post-Rut

In addition to being worn out and hungry, the whitetail has another thing that keeps him from moving about: the constant presence of man. The hunting pressure incurred during September, October and November causes many bucks to become nocturnal. When formulating a hunting strategy for nocturnal post-rut bucks, it's important to understand that all white-tailed bucks are not the same. They fall into two categories, yearlings and adults. This is especially evident in areas where hunting pressure is heavy.

Yearling bucks are much easier to hunt, and it takes a lot of pressure for them to become truly nocturnal.

The sex urge in November's prime breeding season overwhelms most yearling bucks, keeping them constantly on the move. This makes yearlings huntable even in the post-rut. However, if a buck is lucky enough to survive his yearling season, he becomes a totally different animal the second season when he is 2-1/2 years old. These deer, as well as older bucks, really go underground in the post-rut.

Contrary to popular belief among hunters, bucks do not move out of the country when hunting pressure increases. Telemetry studies conducted throughout North America indicate that whitetails do not abandon their core range during hunting season. Bucks simply hunker down, find the thickest cover possible, and limit their movements to nighttime or the fringes of daylight. Couple this with a buck's weakened, rut-ravaged body and it's easy to see why hunting the post-rut is the most challenging time to bag a buck.

▶ Hunting Strategy

I am an opportunist when it comes to hunting right after November's rut. Though some does will be bred

When still-hunting during the post-rut look for small parts of the deer, rather than a whole deer – brown patches, ears or antler tines.

When the post-rut arrives scraping behavior will be only a fraction of what it was during the hot-to-trot rut.

during this time, I know behavior will be much different. I intensely hunt food sources close to thick cover. This is the heart and soul of hunting the late season, or post-rut. By concentrating on food sources and bedding areas, I'm able to get close to doe groups and bucks that have survived to this point in the season. Remember, does, and particularly bucks, need to gain and maintain body weight to survive winter, so everything else takes a back seat to food – even sex.

To be successful, hunting post-rut nocturnal bucks requires that you scout smart for them. For years, I hunted the same way the entire deer season. This amounted to hunting the scrape areas I'd found early in the season. The only thing wrong was that once full-blown breeding arrived and gun season began, scraping activity dwindled to almost nothing. And as gun season progressed, deer sightings decreased significantly.

Then I changed my way of thinking. My buck sightings and opportunities increased dramatically when I began wondering, "If I were a buck, where would I be hiding when the tail end of the season arrived?" As

might be expected, I looked intently at the thickest cover I could find in close proximity to known feeding areas.

▶ Bed and Feed

To save time and energy, I use aerial photos and topographical maps to locate prospective bedding areas. When areas coincide with the topo map's steep elevation lines, it's an indicator of where deer will be bedded. Note that whitetails love to bed just over an edge where they can watch downwind and, and at the same time, have their backs to the wind, enabling them to smell danger in the direction they can't see.

A bedding area's relation to food and water can't be emphasized enough, for it reveals how a buck moves to and from the bedding area. During the post-rut, try to find bedding areas that are close to the whitetail's feeding areas. Bucks are weary and don't want to travel too far for food if they can help it. As a result, you'll often find them bedding in thick cover within 200 to 300 yards of standing field crops or mast sources. If standing corn exists both bucks and does will probably

Few post-rut set ups can compare to hunting in or around corn fields. Any standing corn field at this time of the year will be overrun with deer if cover is available.

Check for fresh rubs during the post-rut because rubbing behavior is still part of a buck's daily routine, though not as intense as during the rut.

During the post-rut, set up near the food source.

Calling during the post-rut can be a very beneficial strategy. Of all the call sounds, I've found the fawn and doe bleat to be the most successful.

buck by being as inconspicuous as possible. This means I do not spend a lot of time in the area. I hang my stand near the bedding area's known escape routes or where sign and cover is thickest. And, I hang my stands as close as I can to known bedding area without spooking deer. In addition, I make sure the stands are hung at least a month before I intend to hunt the area. Because of their size and the amount of noise required to build them, I seldom use permanent stands when hunting nocturnal bucks in thick cover. It's just too risky. If you make too much commotion in the buck's bedroom or close by, he'll move out. With the stand in place, I take time to cut several small shooting lanes. And lastly, I make sure my entrance and exit can be done quietly. This last point is critical.

Though I will not dwell on this a great deal, it's important to note that a whitetail's feeding times in the post-rut can change drastically from what they were prior to November's rut. In the North, where winter usually begins in early December, there will be more activity mid to end of day in the post-rut, especially if hunting pressure has not been intense. In my experience, the hours of 10 a.m. to 2 p.m. and 3 p.m. to nightfall have offered the greatest deer activity during the post-rut.

▶ Post-Rut Breeding Phase

If fawn births are on schedule,

be bedding right in the field.

When a trail is found leading to or from a bedding area, look at the tracks closely. If most or all are heading toward the feeding area, the trail is probably being used late in the day. If the tracks indicate movement into the bedding area, the trail is being used in the morning. Knowing a whitetail's escape routes will help you plan hunting strategies and determine ambush locations.

I plan my ambush of a post-rut

meaning mid-May to early June in the North, and favorable conditions are present in the form of good nutrition, a portion of the doe fawns will come into estrus in December. When the post-rut moon (third full moon after the autumn equinox) is full in the North, there should be some breeding taking place. However, don't expect this to be nearly as spectacular as what took place in November. Unfortunately, by the time the post-rut rolls around, the adult buck population has thinned significantly. As a result, the post-rut breeding phase might not be noticeable, unless more than one buck is vying for the same doe. Then a little chasing may take place.

The thing to remember is that breeding activity is very probable during the post-rut. Concentrate on doe groups because if one doe happens to come into estrus and there are bucks in the area, you'll be in position to take advantage of it. Actually, I don't plan my hunts around this. Instead I concentrate on hunting food and bedding sources where there are concentrations of deer.

▶ Talk'em into Range

The use of antlers and deer calls is associated with hunting the rut. There's no question that November is the time when both work best. However, don't put them away after Thanksgiving, because the post-rut is also a great time to use antlers and calls. Over the years, I've had many close encounters with bucks

ABOVE: Calling during the post-rut can be a very beneficial strategy. Of all the call sounds, I've found the fawn and doe bleat to be the most successful.

RIGHT: These two bucks are two of my best post-rut bucks. I harvested them close to prime feeding areas.

Setting up around apple orchards can be real hot spots during the post-rut.

The Cloverleaf Still-hunt

400 YARDS

The cloverleaf still-hunt: One hunter climbs into a tree stand in the heart of a prime bedding area. Then a lone still-hunter makes a big loop away from the stand hunter and then comes back. When the still-hunter returns to where he can almost see the stand, he makes another loop, continuing the process until he has gone a full 360° around the stand.

because I rattled and called.

When I do rattle during the post-rut, I imitate sparring bucks rather than two that are in a full-blown rumble. Seldom will two bucks try to kill each other after the flurry of the rut is past. So, I find less fighting noise to work better. I might lightly tickle the tines or bang the antlers slowly together. Typically, I do this for less than three to five minutes, in most cases for less than two minutes.

The latter might take place if I can actually see a buck from my stand location. If this happens, I want him to know something is going on in my direction. If he heads for me, I stop the simulated sparring and get ready for the moment of truth.

Set-up is critical when rattling in the post-rut. By being close to the bedding area it isn't necessary to make the sequence loud. But it needs to be loud enough for the bedded buck, wherever he is in the bedding area, to hear it. Also, I don't like to rattle unless I'm in thick cover and have a clear shooting lane downwind from my stand, because bucks often circle downwind as they try to locate the combatants.

Though I love to use antlers in the post-rut, my call of choice is a good grunt tube. I find that grunting and bleating are successful after the rut, and I use the tube the same way I did in October and November.

▶ When the Going Gets Tough

Though stand hunting is my favorite way to hunt the post-rut, silent drives in gun season can also be productive for hunting wary bucks. I'm a loner when it comes to hunting anything, and seldom do I venture into the woods with more than one person. However, late in the season when it appears all bucks have left the country, I like to put on what I call my cloverleaf tactic with another hunter. It works like this.

One hunter positions himself in a tree stand in the heart of a prime bedding area. Then, one lone still-hunter proceeds to make big loops from the stand hunter. The still-hunter hunts away from the stand, makes a big loop, and then comes back. The still-hunter comes back to where he can almost see the stand, then he makes another loop, continuing the process until he has gone a full 360° around the person in the stand. How far out the loop takes the still-hunter depends on the size of the bedding area, but generally the loop takes in the area about 400 yards from the stand. If you were to look at this strategy from above, it would resemble a four-leaf clover, with the stand in the middle. Over the years, I've killed several bucks using this technique. I find it to be a real ace-in-the-hole when post-rut hunting gets tough.

CHAPTER 11

Antlers
What is Realistic?

By virtue of today's information flow, determining top end potential for whitetail antlers in various parts of North America is fairly easy. Assessing what is realistic when it comes to antler size is a bit more difficult for many regions of the country due to a host of factors. Variables such as soil quality, population densities, winter severity and hunting pressure make the determination of what is realistic more complex. Though I will no doubt fall short for some areas, I believe it is possible to provide a good ball park idea of what is realistic when it comes to antler size.

▶ Realistic Size – by Age

What follows comes from years of experience raising and hunting whitetails.

Yearlings (1-1/2-year-old bucks): In my region of the country (western New York State) yearling bucks sport everything from spike antlers to racks carrying six to 10 points. Multi-point yearlings will usually have seven- to 10-inch inside spreads, short tines and score 50 to 80 Boone & Crockett points.

In America's rich farm belts as well as western Canadian farm provinces, few yearlings will carry spike antlers. Most are six- to 10-point basket racks, very similar but sometimes larger than what we have here in western New York.

In areas where the stress of marginal food quality and severe winters are the norm yearlings are often small spikes or fork-horns.

Yearlings in my region have an average live weight of about 120 to 145 pounds. In stressed areas and some southern locations yearling buck weights will average 10% to 20% lighter.

2-1/2-Year-Old Bucks: In most northern and many southern regions a 2-1/2 year-old buck can be very impressive. On average, our 2-1/2 year-old bucks will sport six- to 10- point antlers with a spread of 12 to 14 inches and score anywhere from 85 to 125 Boone & Crockett. Their live weight will be from 160 to 180 pounds. Of course there are many areas of America where 2-1/2 year-olds will be smaller or bigger, but on average these numbers are what I believe to be realistic.

3-1/2-Year-Old Bucks: This age buck can really get a hunter's heart pounding. By the time bucks reaches this age they are finished growing bones and muscle, though they will add muscle mass as they age. If conditions are right, 3-1/2 year-old bucks in most Northern farm regions will carry eight or more antler points, have a spread of 14 to 18 inches and score anywhere from 105 to 150. Their pre-rut live weight will be about 210 to 220 pounds if they are healthy specimens. Of course southern bucks of this age class can be significantly lighter in weight, whereas this age class of bucks in deep woods of Northern Maine can easily weigh 250 pounds on the hoof.

4-1/2+ Year-Old Bucks: By the time most whitetail bucks finish growing their fourth set of antlers they are, in every sense of the word, studs – from body size, to their attitude, to their hat size. Bucks of this age in the northern farm belts will carry antlers of eight points or larger, have 16- to 19-inch-wide spreads and score 120 to 165 Boone and Crockett. On average their pre-rut weight can be 10% to 20% greater than 3-1/2 year-old bucks.

In many areas of North America 80% to 90% of the buck harvest are yearling bucks. Because of this hunting pressure few bucks will ever reach maturity.

▶Reality Check

In the real world, 2-1/2- and 3-1/2-year-old bucks are about the best one can expect to find, at least for the majority of whitetail locales. Why? Because hunting pressure does not allow for older class bucks in most herds. Hunters desiring to hunt truly mature bucks (4-1/2-year-old and older) have to go to areas where deer are managed for age or remote habitats where many bucks can survive to maturity.

Having only 2-1/2- and 3-1/2-year-old class whitetails to hunt should never be viewed as a

The difference between a young and mature buck is significant. On the left is a 2-1/2-year-old and on the right a five-year-old mature 170-inch buck. Without age you will never know what your area's deer herd is capable of producing.

negative. Though both of these age classes are on the front side of full-maturity, they can offer great hunting opportunities. Any hunter fortunate enough to harvest one should feel fulfilled.

Truth be known, a 3-1/2-year-old buck is an incredible rutting machine and a tough creature to hunt. They are equivalent to an 18- to 20-year-old young man who is maxed out on testosterone. In every sense they are a whitetail herd's prime, fine-tuned athlete.

The bottom line is this: never feel slighted by not being able to hunt 4-1/2+ year-old whitetails. There are many reasons why hunters take to the woods each fall, with perhaps the biggest being the enjoyment that comes from hunting a better deer than they have in the past. For many hunters harvesting a 2-1/2-year-old 100-incher is their goal, while others may want to hold out for a 3-1/2-year-old buck whose antlers are knocking on the 140-inch door. Both are great deer and the experience of hunting them is a big part of the

reason we sit for hours in rain, sleet and snow for a chance to harvest one.

▶Top-End Factors

In order for whitetails to graduate to top-end, which means they surpass the Boone & Crockett score of 170, four ingredients (all working together) are required. The four are genetics, nutrition, management (controlling the population), and age. If any of these keys are missing, it will be very difficult for bucks to reach the Boone & Crockett minimum.

Genetics: Much attention is given to the importance of genetics when it comes to big antlered bucks. For the most part North America has great genetics when it comes to whitetails. However, all white-tailed deer are not the same. Not all of the recognized 30 subspecies can be expected to have the same top end. Generally the further north one travels the greater the antler potential. There are several exceptions to this with the most notable being the

The Impact of Age: The next 4 photos show what can happen if a buck can grow to 4-1/2 years of age. This buck was born in a wild, free-ranging herd in western New York State.

It's tough to know what the possibilities are when a buck is a yearling. This is quite typical of a yearling living in good habitat.

By the time the buck reaches 2-1/2 years old he is beginning to show potential. This 122-inch B&C buck would probably be harvested by the majority of deer hunters.

By his third year this buck is really showing promise. At 3-1/2 years of age the buck is done growing his skeletal frame. The buck now scores 150 Boone and Crockett and the best is yet to come.

He's now a heart-stopper and mature in every way. He scores 167 B&C.

South Texas brush country, where body size is smaller than in the northern reaches of the whitetails range but antlers have the potential of rivaling whitetails found in the Canadian provinces.

Nutrition: One of the key ingredients to top-end antlers is health and nutrition. For optimum nutrition to exist, so that whitetails can grow strong healthy bodies, soils need to be optimum and have pH levels of 6.5 to 7.0. In addition the best possible forages and browse need to be present throughout the year but particularly during the critical antler growing months of April through August.

Management: This aspect of the whitetail antler equation is often overlooked. It shouldn't be. When deer populations are not kept in balance with the range's carrying capacity, the health of the animal and antler growth will be affected in a negative way. Also, the stress of too many deer will cause bucks to grow smaller antlers. Due to a multitude of variables it's tough to determine what the antler decline will be from too many deer but it's generally felt among those that raise whitetails that antler growth will be suppressed at least 20% when there are too many deer.

Age: This is the ace card in the deck when it comes to assessing top-end antler potential because if bucks are not allowed to survive to six to eight years of age there is little way of knowing what top-end can be. It used to be thought that top-end antlers occurred between four and five years of age. This is no longer the case. Most successful deer breeders find that antler growth peaks at six to eight years of age.

The bottom line is that truly top-end antlers fall into the fairy tale category for most regions of North America because one or more of the four ingredients for top-end is missing. However, when all are present the results are most impressive.

▶Top-End?

Subspecies and region of the country will dictate top-end antler size. At the risk of slighting an area or being too general I'll offer some sizes to consider. All things being good and equal, whitetail bucks in much of North America can be expected to top out between

140 and 180 inches Boone & Crockett. In my part of New York State (due in part to poorer soils) top-end is about 160 inches. In Canada top-end is a little higher, 145 to 185 inches B&C, due in part to Bergmann's Rule, which states that body size increases the further north a species is found. In some regions there will be exceptions to top-end antlers where some real freak bucks will show up topping 200-inch Boone & Crockett. As impressive as they are, they are exceptions.

Reaching top-end antler growth is no easy feat and requires a host of factors, all working together for it to happen. However, when you understand the process and are fortunate to see such an animal (live or dead) it is a sight to behold.

▶140 Inches – Realistic Top End

Hunters often ask my opinion concerning the size buck they should attempt to harvest on their first trip to a North American whitetail mecca, be it south Texas, Saskatchewan or points in between. Such conversations are interesting because most of these hunters have never placed their crosshairs on any whitetail bigger than a yearling. For the most the part conversations with their outfitters have led them to believe that they should hold out for a buck in the 150- or 160-inch range. There are many areas where such trophies are possible, but not nearly as possible as many hunters are led to believe, especially when hunters are at the mercy of unpredictable weather.

When asked I usually provide two answers after probing a little. For starters I encourage each hunter to hold out for something better than they've killed in the past. I also tell them that regardless of where they go to hunt they will only be there for a short period of time (usually three to six days) and if they've never had the opportunity to kill a 140-inch buck in their life they should seriously consider doing so if the opportunity presents itself. My reasoning is as follows.

I'm a firm believer that a 140-class whitetail buck is a trophy anyplace in North America. I've hunted whitetails from Saskatchewan to Texas to New York and points in between and my experience has taught

Bucks scoring over 200 inches are extremely rare and far from realistic throughout North America. They are equivalent to seeing seven-foot-tall humans.

▶ Antler Characteristics

Deer hunters everywhere get very excited at the sight of bucks carrying antlers that ooze with character. Without question, sightings of bucks with stickers, kickers, drop tines, great inside spreads and heavy mass energize conversations between hunters. How and when these antler bonuses appear is both fascinating and interesting.

Stickers and kickers: Genetics has much to do with sticker/kicker characteristics in a buck's antlers. For some bucks, these protrusions will appear on a buck's first set of antlers. For most bucks, however, stickers and kickers don't begin showing up until after age 4-1/2, when the animal has matured. Usually, the older the buck is the more this trait manifests itself.

On a number of bucks I've raised this characteristic didn't begin showing up until the buck reached 6-1/2 years of age. I had one buck who was either a clean 5x5

me that sightings of bucks with hat sizes greater than 140 inches are few and far between – at least under true fair chase conditions.

There have been many times when I've been in some of the choicest whitetail locations in North America, places capable of producing Boone & Crockett bucks, without seeing a buck that would score over 120 inches. And after photographing hundreds of whitetail bucks in my career I can attest that bucks greater than 140-class are tough to come by and far from the norm. The best analogy I can offer is that a 140- to 145-inch buck is the equivalent of a 6′5″ man. And when you realize that the average height of an American male is 5′10″, you quickly get the picture that a 140-class animal is way above average and very special. Frankly, in the majority of whitetail habitats a 140- to 145-inch buck is as close to top-end as it gets. To expect anything more is wishful thinking.

In most areas of North America this 165-inch buck is realistic top-end.

Look closely at this 140-class buck. In my experience this is what a top-end whitetail would look like in most of North America. Hunting pressure simply does not allow many bucks to carry head gear that exceed 140 to 145 inches

or 6x6 until he was six years old. From that point on things began to get very interesting. When he reached 11 he not only had several stickers but surprised me by growing two matching eight-inch drop tines.

Drop tines: I call drop tines energizers because of the way hunters get excited about them. The predictable thing about drop tines is that they are not predictable. I've seen bucks grow drop tines before they were 4-1/2 years old, and never grow them again. You never know if they will repeat. Drop tines come in all shapes and sizes but in many instances will not

begin showing up until a buck is 4-1/2 or older.

Inside spread: Spread is perhaps the greatest attention getter associated with whitetail antlers. In spite of having nothing to do with the actual antler, a wide inside spread causes a lot of chatter among hunters. For the most part this characteristic will begin showing up in a buck's second set of antlers. If a buck with this genetic trait can make it to full maturity his antlers will literally take your breath away. Nothing makes a whitetail buck's antlers look larger than they really are than a wide inside spread. It should also be

Antlers with a wide inside spread cause a lot of excitement among hunters. Bucks like this 165-inch B&C brute are oddities. The average inside spread of the bucks listed in the Boone and Crockett record book is 17 to 18 inches.

pointed out that bucks with inside spreads greater than 20 inches are oddities. Only one of the many bucks I've raised had an inside spread greater than 20 inches. If you calculate the average inside spreads of all the great bucks in the Boone & Crockett whitetail Record Book you'd probably be surprised to learn that the average is only 17 to 18 inches.

Antler mass: Good genetics must be present but for the most part antler mass is time driven. With few exceptions, truly heavy mass will not begin showing up until a buck reaches 3-1/2 to 4-1/2 years of age and usually peaks around 8 years of age, if the buck can live that long. It should also be pointed out that not all bucks have this genetic trait, though most that reach 4-1/2 years of age will have H-1 (B&C measurement between the burr and 1st point) measurements of 4 to 5-1/2 inches.

The one thing that is predicable about drop tine bucks is their unpredictability. Though very impressive, there is no guarantee that a buck will grow them the following year.

CHAPTER 12

Bagging the Memories

No Alsheimer book on hunting whitetails would be complete without discussing how to hunt with a camera. Cameras don't put venison on the table but they help preserve the experience. This chapter will provide an overview of how I hunt deer with something other than firearms and archery tackle.

Had it not been for the 35mm camera I would not be the deer hunter I am. When I began extending my season by hunting whitetails 365 days a year my whole perspective of whitetails and how they lived took a quantum leap. I wouldn't know a fraction of what I do about the whitetail had it not been for the passion I have for capturing whitetails on film. The bottom line is that the drive to make the best possible photos of whitetails and the hunting experience has helped to keep my life fresh, energized and fulfilled.

It is safe to say that the 35mm camera has defined my career. Others have conveyed their message as a hunter, a writer or just a photographer. I'm one of the few outdoor communicators who was a serious deer hunter long before becoming an outdoor writer and nature photographer. There is no question that my background as a whitetail hunter has helped my outdoor career immensely.

Try to develop an eye for composition. Rather than tight portraits, add the environment and place the animal off center.

Whenever I pick up a magazine or book, the first thing I do is flip through the pages to examine the photos. If nothing catches my eye, I move on. But if a photo grabs my attention, I might spend a considerable amount of time surveying the rest of the book. Though this may sound odd, it really isn't. Scientists tell us that learning is 80% visual, and humans respond more quickly to visual stimuli than anything else. Without the images captured by wildlife photographers, our understanding of the natural world would be considerably less.

Most who make their living as nature photographers say they have the best job in the world. I definitely feel this way, but that doesn't mean it's an easy profession. Believe me, it can be very disheartening at times, especially if you don't know what you are doing.

The essence of wildlife photography is summed up best by my good friend and master whitetail photographer Mike Biggs, who once told me, "Wildlife photography consists of a series of repeated attempts by a crazed individual to obtain impossible photos of unpredictable subjects performing unlikely behaviors under outrageous circumstances." Though a bit humorous, this is, in a nutshell, what whitetail and nature photography is all about.

Due to the whitetail's unpredictable nature, it is impossible to always be successful as a deer photographer. However, a heavy dose of persistence, knowledge of the animal, and the right equipment make it possible to capture great images of America's favorite big game animal.

It's safe to say that wildlife photography has added greater meaning to my life. My quest to get one more photo has often kept me in the woods when I should have called it a day. Through nature photography, I've come to truly appreciate God's incredible creation.

Whenever photographing wildlife, work to do so at the animal's eye level. Also, be sure to focus on the eye, as it is the center of attention.

If water is present, try to get the animal reflected in the photo; doing so will greatly enhance its quality.

I wholeheartedly believe that my mission in life is to photograph the wonders of God's handiwork and share them with others. In large part this is why I do what I do. The other part is that I love it so much.

So, in part I owe my profession and knowledge of the whitetail to photography. Failing to share some tips and the story behind my photos would leave this book with an incomplete ending.

▶ Roots and Tools

My early years were filled with hunting and trapping. When I was twenty and in the U.S. Air Force, I spent a year in Vietnam. While there, I was introduced to the 35mm camera. My motive for buying the camera and assorted telephoto lenses was the opportunity to hunt deer with film when they couldn't be hunted with a bow or gun. After being discharged from the service in 1970, I began to seriously photograph deer and other wildlife. As I soon discovered, the beauty of hunting with a camera is that the season lasts all year and there are no bag limits.

I shoot Nikon cameras and lenses, both film and digital. I currently rely heavily on six lenses: a 12-24mm f4 (digital), 20-35mm f2.8, a 35-70mm f.2.8, an 80-200mm f2.8 VR ED IF, a 500mm f.4.0 AF-S, and a 200-400mm f4.0 VR ED IF. These lenses are extremely sharp (and expensive!) and allow me to photograph when the light is less than adequate. I always try to use the 80-200mm zoom mounted on a tripod or gunstock, though I will shoot it off-hand if lighting permits. The 500mm and the 200-400mm zoom are fairly heavy and are always used with a tripod to ensure that the pictures are as sharp as possible.

▶ Film or Digital?

In case you haven't noticed, photography is changing at warp speed. In the world of nature photography film is still being used by the pros, but this is beginning to change. Due to publisher's demands I continue to shoot the majority of my images on film. However, based on the way things are going I'm sure that within the next couple years I'll be shooting entirely with digital cameras. For this reason I recommend that any new photographers forego film cameras and shoot in the

Lighting is everything when it comes to wildlife photography. Rather than photographing with the light over your shoulder try back or cross light. It will make your photos dramatic.

Always think of using a tripod when photographing whitetails. It will help ensure the images you take are "tack sharp."

digital realm with top-of-the-line cameras that are capable of 6+ megapixels.

Currently I use four-color slide films for the bulk of my photography: Fuji Velvia (ASA 50 & 100) for scenics, Fuji 100 Sensia (ASA 100) for animals, and Fuji 400F Provia (ASA 400) for low-light situations.

I use Fuji Velvia for scenics because it's one of the sharpest films made and its colors are incredible. Fuji Sensia 100 is nearly as sharp as Velvia and records fur colors well. Fuji 400F Provia is my fast-speed film and I shoot it at its ASA rating of 400. I've never used a fast speed film quite like it. It is sharp and holds colors well, and it is excellent in overcast conditions.

As far as film is concerned, it's important to remember a couple things. First, always shoot slide film. In most cases, better prints can be made from slides than with print film. Slides are also easier to scan and are more easily marketed to publishers. Second, slower ASA films will be sharper and have better colors. Unfortunately, everything is a trade-off, and using slow speed film usually means shooting off a tripod.

►Equipment

The digital movement has created a big ground swell, and it looks like film will soon be a thing of the past. Obviously, cameras are vastly different from when I began photographing in the late '60s. Except for the light meter, my first 35mm was completely manual. Today, most of my cameras have all the bells and whistles and are truly state-of-the-art. They are capable of autofocus, can advance the film at nearly six frames per second, offer several programming modes, and have outstanding meter systems. With such incredible technology, it's no wonder that many amateurs are able to get such outstanding photos.

The nature of whitetail photography makes 35mm the format of choice. Whenever someone asks me about what camera I recommend for photographing deer, I ask them how much money they are willing to spend and if they want to use film or digital. Today's cameras are not cheap, be it film or digital. The more features they have, the more costly they are. For the novice to serious amateur, I recommend a medium priced 35mm camera body and a zoom lens in the 35-70mm range. When mounted on a 35mm film camera this lens has a magnification of wide angle to about one and one quarter power and is excellent for scenics (note that the lens' magnification can be calculated by dividing 50 into its millimeter).

By selecting a shutter speed of a 1/15 of a second, motion can be shown in the photo.

Being able to stop the action can make for great photos. Stopping a buck in mid-jump coming right at you requires steady hands, etc.

In order to start photographing deer, a zoom lens in the 80-200mm range is essential. Also, it's best to get the lowest "f" setting you can afford. I have three 80-200mm lenses that are f2.8, and they allow me to photograph in dim light (the smaller the "f" number, the less light required to take a picture). Also, most of today's telephoto lenses offer teleconverters that are matched to the lens. A 1.4 teleconverter only loses 1 "f" stop of light and will make an 80-200mm f.2.8 lens into a 110-280mm f4.0 lens. People often think most deer photos are taken with long lenses. Though many are, the 80-200mm is my workhorse lens and one of my favorites when it comes to "shooting" whitetails.

For the person serious about photographing deer, a 300mm, or better yet a 400mm or 500mm, is a must if you want to reach the hard-to-approach animals. A 300mm (6 power on a film camera), 400mm (8 power on a film camera), or 500mm (10 power on a film camera) will allow you to fill the frame with an animal without taking the risk of spooking it.

Due to the nature of the sensors found on most top-of-the-line digital camera bodies, the magnification of most lenses will be approximately 1.5x greater than when they are when used on film camera bodies. Longer telephoto lenses also are capable of blurring out the background, which is aesthetically pleasing when doing portrait photography.

In most instances, the deer images that grace the covers of major magazines are taken with 300-600mm lenses. The downsides of these lenses are their weight and cost. The weight of most requires the use of a tripod. And the sticker price on these models can make a person cry or tremble, depending on his or her frame of mind. At today's prices, one can expect to pay anywhere from $1,000 to over $6,000 for a top-of-the-line telephoto lens. As with the other lenses, the lower the "f" setting the better your chances of photographing in dim light. Lenses with lower "f" settings will also be the more expensive due to their light gathering capability.

A sturdy tripod is one of the last pieces of equipment required to get into deer photography. Even though it's the last piece of equipment I mention, don't try to cut corners in this area, as the quality of your photos depends on how steady the camera is when you are shooting. To lighten the load, I use carbon tripods. My lightweight model is a Gitzo G1228. My serious tripod – the one I use for my long lenses – is a Gitzo G1325. Both tripods sport a heavy-duty ball head.

Though it isn't as steady as a tripod, a shoulder stock (or gunstock) can help to create sharp photos when you need to be mobile. Both BushHawk and Rue Enterprises market excellent shoulder stocks.

One piece of equipment that isn't necessary but is nice to have for whitetail photography is a portable blind. You can either make your own or purchase one of many on the market. Dollar for dollar, Rue Enterprises' Ultimate Photo Blind (www.Rue.com) is hard to beat. It is lightweight and can be put in place in less than a minute. I've spent countless hours in this blind and have taken some great photos while using it.

▶ Making the Photo

Mark Twain once said, "You can't depend on your eyes if your imagination is out of focus." Though this quote wasn't directed at photography, it could have been. Whenever I conduct photography seminars I emphasize to attendees that their goal should be to "make photos," not "take photos." There is a vast difference between the two concepts. Rather than reacting spontaneously, think creatively when practicing the art of nature photography.

When I first began photographing deer I *took* photos. In the early '70s I was more intent on just getting the deer in the frame than thinking about composition, depth of field, or lighting. All these aspects of photography take time to develop, but with a little knowledge the learning curve can be shortened.

Light is the key to nature photography, and whenever possible, I try to position the deer (or me) so they will not be in direct sunlight. If I have a choice, I like to side-light or back-light my subject. This kind of lighting makes for more dramatic photos; getting it often requires forethought and planning.

Like lighting, the composition of a photo is essential to its appeal. When composing whitetail shots, or photos of any wildlife for that matter, I try to think how the subject will look best. Therefore, I often put the subject off-center in the picture so it becomes a part of the scene. In order to enhance the photo's composition, I'll try to find a tree or some other object to frame the animal. This technique often makes photos much more appealing from an artistic standpoint. To put it another way, I try to have my photos tell a story. This is not to say that I don't like to take tight portraits, because I do. However, I try to get artistic whenever the opportunity presents itself.

When taking portraits of animals, I always focus on the subject's eyes. The eye is the center of attention and reveals the soul and character of the subject. In addition, the glint of the eye adds life to the photo. I also like to take pictures from the subject's eye level. If the subject is a fawn lying on the forest floor, I photograph on my belly.

My best photos usually occur when I go back to a location several times. During the course of photographing, I constantly survey the scene to see which location will provide the best photo opportunities when the sun shines. Because baiting is usually allowed where I photograph, I preplan where

Capture the mood. To get this jumping image required ASA 400 film, which allowed me to shoot at a shutter speed of 640. When an animal is running broadside you don't need as high a shutter speed as when it is coming right at you.

My best buck to date – a 175-inch Saskatchewan Booner. When composing a hunter set-up photo, try to be low to the ground and focus on the object's eyes.

I'll place the bait to get deer in the right position for the photos I want.

Baiting can be done in many forms, and it's wise to find out what is legal where you live. Due to recent deer diseases such as Chronic Wasting Disease, baiting has been banned in some areas. I learned a long time ago that the fastest way to a whitetail is through its stomach. As a result, I use apples and corn to lure deer within camera range. I also use one other device, a deer decoy.

During autumn, white-tailed bucks respond well to a doe or buck decoy. This is especially true during the mating season. I've used decoys extensively and had some incredible experiences with them. If you want to try "deercoying," it's important that a buck be able to spot the decoy, so placing it in an open area is essential. Also, make sure the decoy is anchored to the ground. When a buck approaches a decoy, he often becomes aggressive and if the fake deer isn't anchored it will probably get knocked over, ending the shoot. A word of caution is in order, however. Never use a decoy where hunting is permitted. Today's decoys are works of art and appear very authentic. As a result, from a distance hunters will seldom be able to tell the difference between a decoy and the real thing. So always keep safety in mind.

Perhaps the greatest challenge in nature photography is capturing action. Things can occur fast in the wild, and getting it right doesn't just happen. In order to stop fast movement, you need to shoot a shutter speed of at least a 1/500 of a second, or 1/1,000 of a second if you have enough light. Of course, there will be times when you want to show action by blurring the movement. Creating a sense of motion can be accomplished by shooting at a shutter speed of a 1/15 of a second or slower. The slower the shutter speed, the greater the blur.

▶Where to Make the Photos

Making good deer photos is much easier now than when I broke into the photography business. With urbanization, zoning laws that prohibit hunting, and more and more people raising whitetails, there are numerous opportunities to photograph deer. The trick to all of this is finding out where the locations exist. A good place to start is your state's Department of Natural Resources, which should be able to provide you with a list of individuals who raise deer. Once this has been done, contact some of the farmers on the list to find out if photography is possible at their facilities. In addition, local conservation officers or deer biologists should be contacted to find out if any landowners in your area are feeding deer.

I do a great deal of whitetail photography on our farm and have many blind locations right on our Back 40. When I first began, I relied on photographing in deer wintering areas. Though I still do this, I also photograph on big estates, ranches, national parks (like Smoky Mountain National Park, where deer are used to people), and around metropolitan areas where hunting is limited or prohibited. These locations can be excellent for photography, though cropping cars and houses out of the pictures is sometimes a challenge.

▶Hunter Setups

Photographing whitetails and other animals is what nature photography is all about. However, I love to capture the hunting experience on film because it lets me relive the moment.

When recreating the hunt, think of composing the image in such a way that the environment comes into play. By centering the deer and hunter and framing them with the woods I was able to accomplish this.

ABOVE LEFT: Try to recapture what it was like moments after the kill. Photograph from the animal's eye level and offset the hunter slightly, walking into the frame. ABOVE CENTER: Dawn and dusk offer great photo opportunities. If shooting film, underexpose it by one to two "f" stops to bring added rich red colors to the photo. ABOVE RIGHT: Photograph all aspects of the hunt. Having your camera running in the minutes following the kill will provide you with great memories.

Taking pictures of kill scenes in ways that don't offend people is one of the most overlooked aspects of hunting photography. Showing deer with lots of blood with their tongues hanging out or deer draped on vehicles repulses many people – especially non-hunters – and projects a poor image of deer hunting. So, photographing this aspect of hunting is critical.

Most of my hunter set-up photos are taken with a 35-70mm or 80-200mm zoom lenses attached to a camera body and tripod. The camera's self-timer can be programmed to allow two to thirty seconds between the shutter release and when the photo is taken. It's a great feature for someone who hunts alone and wants to take his own photo.

If I'm hunting alone and need to take a self-portrait, the process is easy. First, I program the camera for the time I'll need to move from the camera to the deer and position myself for the photo. Then, I compose the photo, press the shutter and move to the predetermined spot where I'll appear in the photo.

Angles can mean everything when photographing a hunter walking toward a deer. After the kill, I position a deer where I think it looks best, taking advantage of nice framing possibilities. Then, I usually position the camera a short distance from the buck's head, compose the photo and focus on the buck's eyes. If I want the hunter to be in sharp focus, I make sure the lens' f-setting is at least f8 or higher. If I want the hunter to be slightly out of focus, I'll set the f-setting from f2.8 to f5.6.

If I'm taking a hero shot, of myself or someone else, I make sure there's no blood on the deer. Also, I work the

angles, trying to get the best pose. If I'm photographing another hunter with his deer, I focus on the deer's eyes if it's a fresh kill. If I'm doing a self-portrait, things become more difficult. To make my own picture, I check the scene carefully, noting the height of certain branches around the buck. With this in mind, I compose the photo by using the branches as frames of reference so I don't cut my head off in the picture. I then use as high an f-setting as possible – f8 or higher – so I have a good depth of field, meaning everything is sharp, and take my portrait. It takes time to get used to this, but with practice it becomes rather easy.

It's important to make sure a buck looks like it's a fresh kill. After a buck has been dead for several hours, its eyes glaze and start to become sunken. To remedy this, use a pair of glass taxidermy eyes to make the buck's eyes look fresh. They slip in like contact lenses and can make a buck look like it did moments after it was killed. Also, keep the buck's tongue in its mouth, and keep the mouth closed. If the mouth won't stay closed by itself, force it shut by inserting a small nail through the bottom of a buck's jaw and into its palate.

If I kill a buck just before dark and want to photograph it in daylight the following day, I gut it, clean the hair to remove blood and lay the carcass on pallets overnight. (Laying the carcass on pallets keeps the meat from spoiling.). The next day, I can photograph the buck after inserting glass eyes. And one last thing – don't hang a buck by its antlers if you want to photograph it later. The weight of its body will stretch the neck, and the photos won't appear realistic.

Better Deer, Better Hunting

CHAPTERS THIRTEEN • FOURTEEN • FIFTEEN

CHAPTER 13

Quality Deer Management

For the better part of 15 years, I've been immersed in quality deer management. I'll have to admit there were times in the beginning when I wasn't sure I was doing the right thing. This stemmed from skeptical reactions from fellow New Yorkers and the slow pace of the program's development.

Traditions die hard in the Northeast, and the thought of managing land for quality deer was not an idea that was embraced by many New Yorkers over a decade ago. Despite the drawbacks, I kept the vision. Early on, progress was hard to see. But as the years passed, the QDM philosophy gained both momentum and acceptance when the public was able to see the results.

For decades America's whitetail populations have been managed under a concept known as Traditional Deer Management (TDM). In a nutshell, TDM was used to rebuild America's whitetail herds after the market-hunting era (late 1800s) and is still practiced in many regions of the country today. Though there are a few exceptions, it lets hunters kill any legal antlered buck while protecting all or part of the antlerless population.

One of the foundations of a quality deer management program is letting the young bucks walk and harvesting does so the deer population can be brought in balance with the habitat.

The Alsheimer farm in western New York. In 1973 my wife and I bought this property and set out to turn it into a wildlife paradise. Today, it teems with white-tailed deer, turkeys and a myriad of small game.

Quality Deer Management differs greatly from TDM. It is a philosophy/practice that unites landowners, hunters and resource managers in a common goal of producing biologically and socially balanced deer herds. QDM produces quality does, fawns and bucks. Yearling and 2-year-old bucks are protected to produce mature males, and doe harvesting is emphasized to control the adult-doe-to-antlered-buck ratio. In addition, the practice strives to keep deer habitat at a quality level. QDM also improves landowner relations and creates better hunters. The end result is better habitat, better deer and better hunting.

QDM sounds great, so why doesn't every state agency and hunter want to embrace the concept? Some view it as threatening and others simply resist anything that smacks of change.

▶Understanding

When hunters and landowners watch a well-done presentation on QDM or see the caliber of bucks killed under QDM, their impulse is to jump in and start a program. Land and wildlife management is an energizing experience for some, but it can be a headache for others when they realize what it involves. This is why it's important to understand QDM in terms of land, time, money and equipment before making a decision.

QDM requirements don't have to be overwhelming. Creating quality habitat is like exercising: Anything is better than nothing. Properties of all sizes can benefit from habitat improvement, increased doe harvests and restricted buck harvests.

For some strange reason most hunters/landowners think they have to put together 1,000+ acres to have any kind of a QDM program. Not so. When I decided to walk away from status quo deer management in 1990 our farm was only 185 acres in size. Since that time we've purchased additional land and today we own a little over 200 acres. However, 35 acres of the farm is a high-fenced whitetail research facility, which is off-limits to hunting of any kind. If you back out the house, barns and yard area I wind up managing

My best "farm" buck to date, a 150-class harvested in 2002. Thanks to like-minded neighbors, the quality deer management movement is alive and well in western New York.

about 160-acres for hunting and deer management. So we don't have a large amount of acreage to manage. In spite of limited acreage, the results we've seen have been nothing short of incredible.

When I began in 1990 there was scant information available for small landowners who wanted to implement a QDM program. Because of this I flew by the seat of my pants in the early years. If I knew then what I know now, the ride would have been much less painful, with a much flatter learning curve.

▶Have a Plan

"Failure to plan is a plan to fail." I'm not sure where I heard this the first time but when it comes to having a QDM program a sound plan is the make-or-break ingredient. The better the plan, the better the results will be.

Formulate a plan: When assessing your property step back and take a hard look at its layout, as well as the properties surrounding you. Understand going in that no two properties are the same and your needs and goals are

In order for quality deer management to shine, pressure must be taken off the deer herd. We've found success doing this by limiting our hunting to stand hunting.

Through stand hunting and calling techniques, we've been able to harvest many mature bucks since the early 1990s.

laying out the property's natural habitat, food plots and hunting locations are keys to having success. These locations can't be just any place on your property. They must be in locations that work for you and not your neighbors.

What kind of habitat do you have? Work to make it better. Look closely at the lay of your natural habitat. One of the keys to having a successful quality deer management program is having adequate cover and natural habitat. Deer are thick-cover lovers, the thicker the better. Remember this and remember it well, because it will be a key ingredient in your success or failure.

Having an adequate number of food plots (with the right forages) go hand in glove with natural habitat. For starters at least 5% of a property should be in food plots.

What are your expectations? Be realistic when it comes to antler expectations. If you think you are going to settle for nothing less than a Boone & Crockett size buck you are probably going to have one of two things occur, and maybe both. First, you will never kill such a buck because of hunting pressure on surrounding properties. Secondly (and most hurtful) you will quickly become frustrated by the lack of 140-inch Boone & Crockett bucks in your area. So, for starters try putting all yearling bucks off limits. Once done, try raising the bar each year.

You may find that you'll be satisfied with hunting and killing 100- to 120-inch bucks (usually 2-1/2 year olds). If this is your goal, that's fine. I went through this stage and eventually found that I could pass on the 2-½-year-olds. We now find that hunting and killing 3-1/2+ year-old bucks is possible. We get there by having a minimum 8-point, 16-inch inside spread requirement.

I have one exception to the minimum point/spread rule on our farm. I believe young hunters should not be strapped with minimums. Hunting a whitetail is tough enough without adding antler restrictions for new or young hunters. They simply have too many things to process when they are learning, and forcing them to adhere to seasoned hunter's rules and regulations only discourages their hunting journey.

probably not the same as your neighbors'. As a matter of fact, your neighbors may have no desire to have any deer management/land management plan. If this description fits your neighbors, don't despair. Stay focused on making your own property better.

When I started our QDM program none of my neighbors had a clue that there was a better way of managing deer than what they had been practicing for the previous 50+ years. Today twelve landowners border our farm and only three practice any form of QDM. However, even with so few participants, what we are seeing now, compared to fifteen years ago, is like night and day. To be successful under these conditions with so little land required creative thinking, a great plan, and diligent execution of the plan.

Property layout—what's best for the deer and you?: As you will see in the next chapter,

We've found that when a deer is jumped from its bed, it runs over 400 yards. To keep from pushing deer onto non-QDM neighbor's property we track wounded deer only at night.

For this reason I let my son Aaron kill any buck when he began hunting as a teen-ager. It painlessly let him learn what deer hunting is about. Now that he has a few bucks under his belt (with a couple of dandies harvested), he's passing up younger bucks. I feel certain that without letting him know what it is like to kill a whitetail buck, his enthusiasm for deer hunting would not be what it is.

Controlling the herd: If there are more deer on a property than its habitat can feed, the program will fail miserably. Ideally, an adult-doe-to-antlered-buck ratio of less than 3-to-1 should be strived for. High adult-doe-to-antlered-buck ratios decrease the rut's intensity. Consequently, when the ratio is greater than 3:1, rubbing, scraping, chasing and frenzied rutting behavior greatly diminish.

Most managers consider two adult does per antlered buck attainable. When the ratio is 3:1 or lower, the entire herd benefits because the rut is condensed, fawns are born on schedule and antlered

bucks experience less stress.

A liberal antlerless harvest is often needed to maintain a desirable doe population. Next to limiting the buck harvest, a restricted doe population is the most critical step in a successful QDM program.

Develop a hunting strategy: I'll expand on this later but basically you must resign yourself to the fact that drive and still-hunting techniques are gone forever if you wish to have any kind of quality deer management success on acreages under 300 acres. I've found that when you jump a deer it normally runs or walks up to 400 to 600 yards before stopping. On smaller land parcels this usually means the buck is off your property before he stops, leaving him at the mercy of non-QDM neighbors. Because of this, stand hunting is the way to go.

Limit human activity on the property: Whitetails may not have the same intelligence level as black labs but they are incredibly smart

Our goal is to graduate bucks to 3-1/2 years of age. This age class is mature and adds to the quality of the hunt.

and they learn fast. If you think for a moment you can run ATVs all over a property smaller than 300 acres and not turn them nocturnal, you're just kidding yourself. The fewer people you have running around the property, the more daytime deer activity you will have.

Keep records: You'll never know where you are going unless you know where you've come from. Don't leave things to memory; keep records of what you are doing. If you don't you won't possibly know if you are being successful. It's important to know if your deer are getting larger or digressing. At the very least you should know live weights and the age of all deer harvested on your property.

▶Selling the QDM Idea

Anyone who has ever tried QDM will be quick to tell you that it is the best, most exciting way to manage whitetails. So, if this is the case, why are there still skeptics? I'm convinced that the skeptics have either been pitched the idea in a condescending way or haven't been shown how QDM can benefit everything it touches—from the deer to the habitat to the hunter. Teamwork among friends and neighbors is required for QDM to be effective. Salesmanship is equally important.

In my writings and lectures, I often share the saying, "Nothing happens until something is sold." Those who practice QDM quickly realize that managing deer is much easier than managing people. Deer can be controlled, but people are another story because they have minds of their own and more often than not, they resist change.

Convincing friends and neighbors that QDM will work takes a well-prepared game plan that is wrapped in a blanket of salesmanship and sensitivity. At the grassroots level, a socially acceptable plan should be:

1) Highly organized;

2) Designed for the long term;

3) Able to keep the fire lit among participants;

One of the backbones of our program has been increased doe harvesting. Since we began doing so the quality of our deer herd and hunting experience has increased dramatically.

4) Capable of setting a good example for those not yet participating;

5) Free of pushy tactics to promote the concept; and

6) Able to embrace and educate neighbors.

▶ Be Organized

The best salespeople have a vision and a plan. Having a plan is critical when selling QDM to neighbors and other hunters. The benefits of quality deer management must take center stage, and the idea that QDM always works when it is given a chance must be emphasized. It's hard for the public to refute better habitat, more mature bucks, a more balanced sex ratio and better hunters in the field. If people can be introduced to this in a non-threatening way they will buy it.

▶ Set a Good Example

Remember that selling QDM will take time. Rome wasn't built in a day, and getting the public to embrace

QDM doesn't happen overnight. It's important not to hurry the process. Win the public's trust with facts, results, and a heavy dose of kindness.

The phrase "more is caught than taught" often applies to raising children, but it is also true in QDM. Setting a good example for fellow hunters can be far more convincing than lecturing them on whitetail management.

One of the worst things you can do during a QDM sales pitch is to force the concept on people. It won't work! Save your energy, because people – especially hunters and country folk – don't like to be told what to do or that what they're doing is wrong.

Being pushy irritates people. As Kenny Rogers sang, "You have to know when to hold 'em and know when to fold 'em." It's important to know when and how to play your QDM cards. By breaking down the concept and presenting it in bite-size pieces, you'll be more successful. However, even though it's wise to slowly introduce someone to QDM, make sure you're

Managing a property for quality deer, habitat and hunting has united local landowners in becoming better stewards of the land God has entrusted to us.

consistently promoting the concept. QDM is a yearlong endeavor – it cannot shut down when deer season ends. Convincing landowners to start a QDM program is just the beginning.

▶ Love Thy Neighbor

Having a positive relationship with your neighbors is not always an easy thing to do, especially if they are resisting change. QDM can create conflicts between adjacent landowners. Just like design and implementation, effectively dealing with these conflicts is important for a successful QDM program. If bickering occurs, a program can be seriously affected.

Conflicts between neighbors and hunters within a group can range from simple to complex. Most problems are minor at first, but they can easily escalate into major confrontations. It doesn't take much for a minor misunderstanding to turn into a border war.

One of the best ways to convert neighbors to QDM is through education. The Quality Deer Management Association (www.qdma.com) is a great organization that disseminates all kinds of information on the subject. I'm convinced that if hunters had to go through an education and sensitivity course, the process of selling the QDM concept would be much easier.

BENEFITS OF QDM

- Deer population doesn't exceed property's carrying capacity
- Improved buck-to-doe ratio
- Older age-class of bucks
- Improved habitat
- Better hunting
- Better landowner/hunter opportunities
- Better understanding of property's ecosystem
- Feeling of accomplishment

The sign on the post reads:

POSTED
PRIVATE PROPERTY
HUNTING, FISHING, TRAPPING OR
TRESPASSING FOR ANY PURPOSE
IS STRICTLY FORBIDDEN
VIOLATORS WILL BE PROSECUTED

CHAPTER **14**

Build it and They Will Come

I receive many questions as a traveling seminar speaker. Attendees want to know a host of things about the white-tailed deer, from how to hunt them to how to feed them. When I first hit the seminar trail twenty-five years ago hunters were primarily interested in how-to hunting strategies. No more. Today, one of the most frequently asked questions is, "How do you lay out your property and make it attractive to deer?"

There is no question that the face of hunting is changing. Today's hunter is more management-conscious than at any other time in the history of American hunting. Soil composition, food plot layout and deer nutrition now dominate discussions.

▶In The Beginning

I wish I could tell you my first experience with land management and food plots was the perfect model. It wasn't – far from it. When my wife and I purchased our farm in the fall of 1973 I immediately planted my first food plot. Though adequate for the times, it was a far cry from what we do now. During the last 30+ years I've worked to refine our land management practices. It's been an interesting journey, one worth sharing.

During the winter months, consider cutting cull trees to provide browse.

Consider selective cutting in the designated sanctuary. By making a sanctuary thick with tree tops and secondary growth deer will prefer to bed there.

▶ Goals

Before the first clump of dirt is turned thought must go into what you want to accomplish. Doing land management and food plots is far more than looking at an open patch of land and saying, "It won't take much effort to put my food plot there."

First and foremost the process needs a plan. Since 1990 I've made a concerted effort to think through what I want to accomplish. In 1990 I traveled to Texas where I met with legendary quality deer management pioneer Al Brothers. What he shared with me regarding land management, deer management and food plots changed my way of thinking. Prior to this I gave little thought to layout and managing our property for quality deer. I do now.

There's almost no resemblance between the way I did our land and food plot management prior to 1990 and the way I manage it now. Unlike pre-1990, when I planted food plots wherever the land lay right, today I lay out my food plots so they work in concert with the natural habitat. The bottom line is that the current program offers better deer and better deer hunting.

How I've been successful turning a 200-acre property into what I consider a great hunting location has not been that difficult. It simply required a plan and an understanding of the habitat needed and the animal.

▶ Property Layout

Laying out a property for quality deer management is the foundation of any program. Very few (if any) properties are tailored for QDM, either when they are purchased or when the decision is made to manage for quality deer and deer hunting. Sometimes all that is required to make a property QDM friendly is minor tweaking, but often major work is required. The process is like building a house. If a property is built right deer will not only come, but stay. The goal should be to build the best-managed deer mecca possible.

Initially, when we purchased our farm it consisted of 90 acres of mature hardwoods, 25 acres of brush and 65 acres of open fields. To accomplish our goal of making the farm more attractive for deer, turkeys, and grouse, I knew a make-over was in order. I can remember framing a large aerial photo behind glass and, with the aid of a grease pencil, marking it up, trying to come up with the best layout.

QDM was unheard of at the time, so I didn't understand deer management as I do today, but I did know that the wildlife I was interested in needed more and better cover. By "dreaming" on the glass that covered the aerial photo, I broke the bigger fields into small one- to seven-acre sections, with some earmarked for evergreens and shrub plantings. The layout called

Deer will use the sanctuary as their primary bedding area. The key is to stay out of the sanctuary during the hunting season.

A deer management program must have natural habitat available to the property's whitetails.

for some of the evergreens and shrubs to be planted in blocks and some into hedgerows. Other openings were projected as food plots. In the first two years we planted thousands of trees and shrubs, which over time drastically changed the farm's appearance.

Needless to say I've learned much in the last 20+ years. Along the way there were more challenges with the biggest being how to hold deer on the property. Others included how to set up the property for the best hunting opportunities, how to give the deer the foods they need and how to keep young deer that need to grow older from being killed by non-QDM landowners. To accomplish these goals it was important for food plot locations to be set up so that our deer did not have to travel from surrounding properties to take advantage of them. This was and is being done by providing wind friendly setups (for the hunter) and the thickest possible cover near each food source.

▶The Wind Factor

When mapping out a property for QDM practices, always think in terms of how you will hunt it when the sanctuaries and food plots are in place. The goal is to be out of a deer's sight and mind, which ultimately means out of its nose. For this reason never place a food plot in such a fashion that a deer will smell you as it exits its sanctuary when coming to feed.

For best results, lay out the hunting sites for cross winds and work hard to ensure that there will be no swirling winds at the ambush site. In addition, lay out the hunting plot so that the hunter doesn't have to look into a rising or setting sun when it comes time to kill a deer.

▶Build a Sanctuary

"Thicker is better" is a phrase often used to describe what it takes to hold deer on a property. Few think of this, but it is important to set up safe havens for individual doe groups. If you can hold several different doe groups on a property you can hold the bucks. This can be accomplished by creating

Forest management will enhance the healthy trees. When a forest is nurtured, trees such as oaks will produce more mast. Below, is an example of one of my favorite food plot hunting locations. The brush pile behind the stand prohibits deer from going down wind.

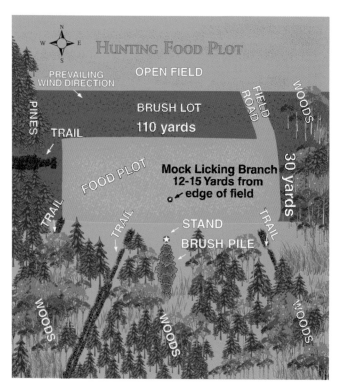

In our region of the country nearly half of a whitetail's diet consists of natural habitat. For this reason we strive to produce as much natural habitat as possible. This buck is feasting on wild grapes.

When food, cover and safety are provided, whitetails will prefer to stay on that property. In turn, hunting opportunities increase with stay-at-home bucks present.

We've worked hard to have a successful apple orchard on our property. Rather than removing the prunings we leave them for deer to browse on.

10 STEPS TO BETTER HABITAT

1. Improve woodlots through carefully planned timber and deer harvests.
2. Consult a professional forester and explain your goals. Determine whether you are interested in creating wildlife habitat or maximizing timber production.
3. With a plan in place, have the forester mark the trees to be cut. Be sure to leave enough mast-producing trees so deer have a constant food source.
4. Develop a contract and put the timber up for bid.
5. If you live in the North, try to have the cutting done in winter to keep forest scarring to a minimum. Treetops should be left in the woods because they provide food and cover for wildlife and enhance forest regeneration.
6. Supplement natural browse by planting shrubs and fruit and mast-producing trees in strategic locations. Be sure to protect young trees from browse damage by using tree tubes or wire cages.
7. Prune fruit trees for optimum production. Do the pruning during the winter and leave the pruned branches on the ground for deer browse.
8. Fertilize fruit and mast-producing trees with 15-15-15 fertilizer. Make four to eight six-inch-deep holes with a steel bar under the tree's drip line and fill the holes with fertilizer in early spring.
9. Kill enough antlerless deer to minimize over-browsing.
10. Formulate a long-range plan to ensure that your natural habitat produces enough food to feed deer year-round.

multiple sanctuaries, areas that are totally off limits to hunters. If you break down and hunt a sanctuary when the hunting gets tough, you've defeated your purpose. Learn this and learn it well because it will be one of your biggest tickets to success. At the very least 25% of a property should be placed into a sanctuary habitat, and much more if possible.

When I first began practicing QDM on our farm in 1990 I had one 40-acre sanctuary. It didn't take me long to realize there was a better way. Over the years I learned that the greater the acreage in sanctuaries the greater the whitetail potential would be. Today our farm has about half of its 200 acres designated as sanctuary, with their size ranging from five to fifty acres.

If a thick sanctuary set-up does not already exist, I'll often encourage a landowner to cut less desirable cull trees within a three- to five-acre area in order to develop a sanctuary. In five or six years such locations should see good regeneration, which will provide the sanctuary cover deer need. The goal is to have available natural browse, thick cover up to six feet off the ground, and not be able to see more than 60 yards through the brush or woods. This kind of cover is required to hold deer.

In the majority of cases a professional forester should be hired to ensure that proper forest management practices take place. When consulting with a professional forester, make sure that they know in detail what you want to accomplish. By having a forest management plan you will help ensure that the whitetails roaming your property have the natural food sources they require.

Though natural habitat requirements vary by region of the country it is not uncommon for over half of a whitetail's diet to come from natural food sources. The accompanying browse analysis study on page 146 was conducted at our research facility and illustrates the importance of providing whitetails a variety of browse species.

If a sanctuary plan calls for reforesting an open field, think about planting fast- to moderate-growing trees and shrubs. I've had great success using

Having soft mast available to a property's deer greatly enhances both the herd and hunting opportunities.

staggered rows of evergreens and shrubs for such sites. In the long run, staggering the species will produce much thicker cover.

Though the role of food plots will be covered in the next chapter it should be pointed out that any road in a forest setting should be considered for a food plot if it runs north and south and can get four to five hours of sunlight during the day. This can be attained by cutting back the edges of the roadway fifteen to twenty yards on either side. Each mile of forest road has the capability of producing a one-acre food plot. This kind of forest food plot offers deer the ultimate security when they want a convenient snack.

▶Food Plot Layout

Security and forage requirements should play an important role in laying out locations for food plots.

Security: Don't even think about planting a food plot where it is visible from a public road or a neighbor's property. Doing so will probably mean that your prized deer will be killed before you get a chance to hunt them. If you must utilize a field next to a public road for a food plot your only option is to plant a shrub hedge along the road. Shrubs will grow fast and create a barrier so deer won't be poached from the road.

If a prime food plot location borders a neighbor's wooded area, be forewarned that the deer will feed on your land but bed on your neighbor's land, which means you will be feeding them and your neighbor will be killing them. So work hard to lay out both feeding and hunting food plots so that deer will not be exposed to the "outside" world, but will be close to bedding areas and

Browse Analysis: Steuben County, New York

Since 1995, I have fed the deer in my enclosure a variety of natural browse species daily for two reasons. First and foremost, the mixture provides a balanced diet. Second, it helps to determine which natural foods are preferred.

The accompanying table details the natural browse my deer prefer, along with two well-known tree species they eat when nothing else is available. After we collected leaves and browse on our farm, we sent samples to the NEAS Diagnostic Laboratory in Cornell University in Ithaca, New York, for protein and fiber analysis.

There are two things to remember when looking at the analysis. First, after years of analyzing browsing behavior, it is apparent that deer don't necessarily gravitate to high-protein foods. If they did, striped maple would be a preferred food. My enclosure deer, as well as the free-ranging deer on our farm, won't touch it, regardless of the time of year.

Second, as the year progresses, a deer's desire for leaves decreases if more preferred foods are available. This behavior becomes evident near mid-July. By mid-August, leaf consumption nearly ceases, especially if acorns are plentiful.

Like humans, whitetails eat what smells and tastes best to them, even when the nutritional value is not as high as other foods. I've even seen deer prefer foods the other deer in their group don't like. For example, I have a 6-1/2-year-old buck that loves American beech browse, while most of the enclosure deer prefer other browse. One thing is certain, though. All deer love ash, wild apple and basswood despite varying protein levels. Based on my observations, it is apparent there is more at work than nutrition, at least in terms of crude protein and fiber.

Note: The May samples were gathered in mid-May 2001 at leaf-out. The August samples were gathered in mid-August 2001 when deer stopped eating leaves. The December samples were cut in mid-December 2001. All samples came from my whitetail research facility in the Town of Avoca, Steuben County, New York. The first percentage in the table represents crude protein and the second represents crude fiber.

Highly Preferred Species in Order of Preference
(Percentages represent crude protein and crude fiber respectively)

Species	May 15, 2001	Aug. 15, 2001	Dec. 15, 2001
1. Wild Apple	3.8%-5.6%	11.7%-12.3%	4.2%-19.7%
2. Basswood	6.1%-4.3%	6.9%-7.4%	3.4%-20.2%
3. Ash	4.8%-6.7%	6.7%-11.4%	3.3%-30.7%
4. Aspen	9.1%-12.9%	6.1%-9.3%	5.1%-17.6%
5. Hard Maple	7.0%-8.8%	4.8%-9.8%	4.6%-25.7%
6. Red Oak	5.6%-7.5%	6.8%-11.3%	3.0%-31.7%
7. Staghorn Sumac	6.3%-4.1%	7.5%-4.0%	6.0%-28.0%
8. Raspberry Plants	5.0%-5.4%	N/A	N/A
9. Black Cherry	13.4%-12.8%	5.9%-7.1%	3.2%-18.2%
10. Wild Strawberry	3.1%-4.1%	N/A	N/A

Nonpreferred Species – Eaten if Other Browse Is Unavailable

11. American Beech	7.4%-12.7%	7.8%-13.2%	4.3%-23.6%
12. Striped Maple	9.8%-8.6%	2.5%-3.5%	2.4%-20.4%

Highly Preferred Winter Food*

1. White Cedar	N/A	N/A	4.2%-12.7%
2. Hemlock	N/A	N/A	3.6%-11.2%

* White cedar and hemlock are highly preferred by my enclosure deer and by wild deer during winter. Their preference for these two types of browse at this time of the year rivals their preference for the four top-preferred foods on the above list. However, white cedar and hemlock are not browsed much, if at all, during the rest of the year.

Making a property more attractive to whitetails ensures greater hunting opportunities.

I harvested this great 8-pointer on our farm at the very end of our 1999 season as it was trying to breed a doe fawn.

sanctuaries. By being close to sanctuaries the deer will not have to travel far to get to them.

Forage Requirements: Every deer on your property requires at least one to two tons of nutritional food a year to meet their needs. If you don't provide it for them, they will go elsewhere. For this reason a minimum of 5% of a property should consist of good food plots, both feeding and hunting.

The difference between the two is that feeding food plots are larger, so they provide the tonnage deer need to thrive and stay on the property. Hunting food plots are smaller and located in thick cover, between the bedding/sanctuary and large feeding area. Hunting food plots should be narrow, irregularly shaped, and less than 1/2 acre in size so that bow shots can be taken across them.

The beauty of hunting food plots is that they provide deer with a fast-food stop as they travel between their bedding and feeding plot. Because hunting food plots are small, with security around them, deer will hit them during daylight. Feeding food plots on the other hand are intentionally large so they can produce the tonnage needed. Deer will normally use feeding food plots under the cover of darkness because of their size and layout.

CHAPTER 15

Better Food Plots

Turning our small property into a great hunting location has basically required nothing more than a keen understanding of what whitetails need to survive. In many ways, deer are what they eat. With this in mind I'll provide the step by step process I go through to ensure the deer roaming our farm have the high quality nutrition they require to reach their potential.

▶ Get the Stones Right

Plants that deer feed on are for the most part nothing more than the delivery device for the nutrients in the soil. Consequently, it is critical to get the soil's pH as good as possible to ensure optimum food plot success. Over the years I've worked diligently to improve our soil's pH before the first seed is planted.

Due to our farm's soil structure we've had to apply many tons of lime to get the food plot location's soil pH over 6.0. Though it's best to get the soil to a pH of 7.0 (neutral) it simply isn't possible in many parts of America. However, if a soil pH of 6.0 to 7.0 can be attained, great food plots can be grown.

How Soil pH Affects Plant Production	
Soil pH	**Approximate Plant Productivity***
7.0	95%
6.5	85%
6.0	70-80%
5.5	45-55%
5.0	15%
4.5	10-15%

*Note that this will vary, depending on forage, soil type and rainfall.

One goal of food plots is to provide supplemental feed. They also provide great hunting opportunities.

Before you plow the first furrow, you should have a soil test completed to determine alkalinity. For less than $20, you can have a farm co-op or the county cooperative extension conduct a soil analysis to determine mineral needs. Collecting the soil for this test is not a difficult process. Merely scoop four or five small samplings of dirt (five inches deep) from the corners and center of the plot then mix all the extracted soil in a bucket. Once done, take or send a sandwich bag of the mixed sample to the lab for testing.

▶ Pre-Plan Soil Prep

To insure your seed selection has a fighting chance to grow spray the food plot location with an herbicide such as RoundUp prior to tilling. It kills all the grasses and weeds and within a week or two the site will turn brown and be ready for tilling.

Once the herbicide has done its job the soil can be turned. Many use plows or disks to accomplish this. Though both will work fine, I prepare food plot sites using a commercial grade roto-tiller. I attempt to do this just prior to a rain front arriving so that the plot can be planted a day or so before rain. It isn't always possible but I have had a fair amount of success by being a weather watcher.

After the earth is turned the tilled area's surface is smoothed (and lime added, if needed) in preparation for planting. This can be done easily by floating the surface with an 8´x8´ piece of weighted cyclone fence.

Because none of our farm's food plots are larger than three acres in size, the next step in our process is to hand-broadcast the selected seed over the site. Once the seed has been properly broadcast, I apply the suggested amount of fertilizer with a fertilizer spreader.

With seed and fertilizer in place, the food plot's seed is packed into the ground. Though a cultipacker might work better, I have a good tractor-pulled roller to do this step.

Rain is the linchpin to successful food plots. Getting a good, soaking rain shortly after a planting works wonders. If rain doesn't come shortly after a plot has been planted, weeds have a way of rearing their ugly heads. Consequently I've always tried to plan my planting around times when rain is forecast.

▶ Forage Selection

I base my forage offerings on our deer's nutritional needs. Because we have snow cover from January through March, I have to do meal planning for nine months. This requires that some plots be planted in

A commercial-grade tiller allows us to preserve soil and sculpt plots to the shape we desire.

The foundation of great food plot management is having the best soil possible. In many regions of the country the only way to raise soil pH is by liming. Over the years we've applied tons of lime to ensure that our food plots produce.

bites they take of each forage being tested.

It's been fascinating to see the way whitetails go from plant to plant to make their forage selection. In many ways it's like watching and keeping track of what humans select at a restaurant salad bar. Though labor-intensive, the study has been very revealing.

The bottom line is that all forages available to food plot practitioners are not equal, not by a long shot. This is because many of the forages offered today were initially developed for cattle. Though cattle and deer are both ruminants they have different requirements when it comes to forage. Consequently, if you want the best value for your dollar it is important to use only forages specifically developed for deer.

Three forages we've done a lot of work with are clover, chicory and brassica, which are extremely popular today. On average all will provide three to six tons of high nutrition forage per acre. What we've discovered is that during the prime growing season nothing trumps whitetail-engineered clover. The accompanying side bar compares clover, chicory and brassica and shows our deer's preference for them during different stages of the growing season.

For further analysis the following is a breakdown for four of the more popular food plot seed choices. It should be noted that all clover, chicory and brassica seeds are not engineered for white-tailed

the spring and some in late summer in order to provide the nutrition deer need.

Over the years we've done many interesting studies in our 35-acre fenced white-tailed deer research facility, which I've written about in my books and magazine articles. One ongoing study deals with

forage preference.

By contour planting a variety of annual and perennial forages I've been able to see which forage deer prefer most. To determine this, our facility's deer are released into test sites and allowed to select the forage they want. While they feed we keep track of how many deer. The key is to use only whitetail engineered seeds. So, before purchasing and planting any of these it is important to know the track record of each.

Clover: When it comes to feeding white-tailed deer, perennial clover is tough to beat, providing the seed used is a variety that has been specifically engineered for whitetails. Great clover plots can be grown if the soil has a pH of 6.0 or higher. During the prime growing season, clover can be expected to have protein levels that exceed 25%, producing four to five tons of high nutrition per acre.

With proper mowing and spraying, perennial clover food plots are capable of lasting four or five years.

Chicory: Chicory is a perennial forage and often referred to as "clover on steroids." It is drought resistant, highly digestible to deer and on soils with a pH higher than 6 to 6.5 it is capable of providing four to five tons of highly nutritious forage per acre. Chicory also has the ability to transfer minerals from the soil better than clover and performs much better than clover when dry conditions exist. Its protein levels generally run in the 20% to 25% range.

Brassica: Brassica is an annual and a very popular whitetail forage choice in both southern and northern settings. In the South it grows well in dry conditions and is graze-tolerant. In most southern locations, deer will begin feasting on it when it is three to four inches tall.

In the North, brassica has proven to be an incredible late autumn/early winter forage for whitetails and begins being attractive to northern deer after it has experienced several frosts. Frosts cause the plant's starches to turn to sugar. During the summer the plant's protein

Hand broadcasting seed is a great seeding method for plots of 5 acres or less.

Our ongoing forage research project has allowed us to let the deer in our enclosures tell us what they prefer to eat.

Forage Preference

It is critical to note that during the months when deer are growing their antlers, they prefer and are eating whitetail-engineered clover.

	Whitetail Engineered Clover	Chicory	Brassica
MAY	10	0	0
JUNE	8	2	0
JULY	7	3	0
AUGUST	6	4	0
SEPTEMBER	8	2	0
OCTOBER	6	3	1
NOVEMBER	4	3	3
DECEMBER	2	1	7

During the antler-growing season, it is critical to provide forages that can deliver 20% protein. Few things can trump whitetail-engineered clover.

If you have the ability to plant multiple food plots, corn might be an option. A downside of corn is that over half of it will be utilized by non-deer species and it doesn't normally last long if a lot of deer are eating it.

During the lactating period, high-octane food must be available to does and fawns.

levels exceed 30% and still exceed 20% to 25% in the winter. It is highly digestible and, depending on soil type, can provide three to four tons of forage per acre during the growing months.

Corn: Corn is an annual forage that many food plot practitioners attempt to plant. Though corn is highly preferred by whitetails (6% to 8% protein and high in carbohydrates) it cannot provide the long-term nutrition deer require. Many refer to it as a "one month wonder" because its availability to deer is only about 30 to 45 days once it matures. Also, roughly 60% of the crop will be consumed by non-deer species such as birds, raccoons, squirrels and bears. In addition, it is harder to grow than the other three forages mentioned.

However, under the right circumstances corn does have a place when it comes to food plot offerings. If you have a number of different food plot forages you are working with, corn can provide diversity. It is drought-resistant and high in carbohydrates that convert to fat and can provide a great late-season food choice for deer.

If you want to plant corn the soil pH should be 6.2 or better. Generally corn plants should be eight inches apart; seeds planted 1-1/2 to two inches deep, with a planting rate of 28,000 to 30,000 seeds per acre. The ground temperature should also be 50° F or higher before planting.

▶ When to Plant

Because our part of the country sometimes goes from winter to summer without seeing anything that resembles spring, I've come to realize that my best food plots are the ones planted in early August when the ground temperature is excellent and late summer/early autumn rains occur on a regular basis. I strive to do this planting the last week in July or the first week in August. Note that it takes roughly 45 days to get plants big enough

If you intend to hunt a food plot it should be less than a half-acre in size and shaped so that a bow shot can be made across it.

for deer to utilize them. By planting around August 1, deer are able to begin utilizing the plot's forage by September 15.

Spring planting is preferred by many food plot practitioners. The key is to make sure that the ground temperature exceeds 50° F to 55° F (in the North) before working the soil. One of the difficulties I've had with spring planting is that any residual weed seed that is on the ground tends to grow at a faster rate than the desired forages planted. These weeds can be tough to deal with by mid-summer and aggressively compete with forages like clover or chicory.

▶ Food Plot Maintenance

Food plot maintenance is one area of land management that is often overlooked. Never assume that perennial forage will just grow and grow and grow. Even the best seed requires seasonal maintenance.

Frost-seeding: To keep my clover and clover/chicory food plots prime, I frost-seed existing plots each spring with a light application of the particular seed. Frost-seeding guarantees that I have a lush plot from year to year. It also allows me to get four years or more out of them.

Mowing: One of the best ways I control weeds and maintain the highest nutritional levels in my clover and clover/chicory food plots is by frequent mowing. When these plots reach a height of 12 to 14 inches I mow them back to eight inches high. If you allow clover to get much taller than this, weeds take hold and the nutritional level begins to drop. By keeping my clover plots in the eight- to 12-inch range I know that I can keep the protein levels above 20%, which is what I strive for.

I'm careful to not mow when the plots are stressed by heat and drought and often schedule mowing when I know rain is coming. In addition, I never mow the entire clover food plot all at once.

An exclosure should always be set up in a food plot to see how much the deer are using the plot.

Forages such as brassica can deliver high nutrition long after forages such as clover are covered with snow.

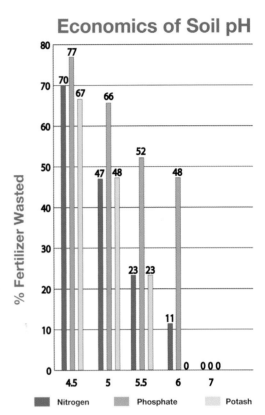

Economics of Soil pH

% Fertilizer Wasted

Nitrogen ■ Phosphate ■ Potash ■

Liming and pH

This chart, prepared from the Mississippi Department of Wildlife, Fisheries and Parks, shows the importance of soil pH. When the pH drops below neutral, or 7.0 pH, fertilizer effectiveness decreases, thus illustrating the benefits of liming.

Rather, I mow a third to one half of a given plot at a time. Understand that when you mow you stress the plant. So by mowing a little at a time I can keep part of the plot attractive to the deer using it. After four or five days I return and mow the rest of the plot, which allows the previously mowed section time to recover.

Spraying: Herbicide maintenance is critical for food plots. Right after spring green-up, I spray my clover food plots to kill the grasses and weeds. I make every attempt to do this before the grasses and weeds get six inches high. If they get higher than this they will be tough to kill. Specifically I use Vantage for the grasses and Pursuit for selected broadleaf weeds. If we have a wet summer I may spray a second time.

Fertilizer: All of my perennial food plots get a fertilizer "drink" twice a year, once just after spring green-up and another in late August or very early in September. One of my goals is to provide our deer with the nutrition and tonnage of forage they need. Fertilizer allows the plants to be fed so my goals can be reached. Of course the blend of fertilizer I use is dictated by the forage that is planted and the soil's requirements.

▶Equipment

Economics and need have dictated the kind of

In 2003 I passed twice on this buck during our gun season, when it was a 2-1/2-year-old, 115-inch eight-pointer. During the winter I found his sheds in our sanctuary. Throughout the 2004 summer months he fed in ours and the neighbor's food plots and was captured on trail cameras. Throughout the 2005 bow season I hunted hard but never saw him. Then, on our gun opener, I was fortunate to harvest him when he came to check out one of my mock scrape's licking branches.

equipment I've used over the years.

Spraying: Though I've never used ATV equipment for constructing my food plots, I do use a John Deere Gator for farm maintenance and food plot spraying. A 15-gallon portable sprayer equipped with a boom allows me to spray one acre at a time.

I started my food plot career 31 years ago with a Ford 601. This tractor served me well but because it was only a little over 20 horsepower it didn't quite have the power I needed to meet my goals. Now I have a 39-horsepower diesel tractor, a four-wheel drive John Deere 4510. I find this size tractor to be just the ticket for all my food plot needs.

Soil Prep: Though I have a set of plows and a good set of disks I try to construct my food plots with a six-foot-wide, heavy-duty, tractor-driven tiller whenever possible. This is an incredible piece of equipment that allows me to sculpt the shape of the plot while at the same time get into tight places. It is also much faster than using a plow and disk.

Mowing: I accomplish my entire food plot mowing with a six-foot-wide, tractor-pulled mower that some might refer to as a bush-hog. I always mow with the tractor's engine at high RPMs so the mower's blades rotate fast enough for cleaner cutting.

My excursion into land management and food plots has been a journey that continues to evolve. It's a process that has made me appreciate the land while at the same time giving back more than I started with. The process has been extremely fulfilling. I can't think of a better way to help steward what God has entrusted to us.

What Matters Most

CHAPTERS SIXTEEN • SEVENTEEN • EIGHTEEN

CHAPTER 16

My Journey

Recently a newspaper reporter asked me to reflect on my career as a writer, hunter and wildlife photographer. As I considered how to respond my thoughts focused on how my incredible journey began. What I've accomplished as a writer and photographer has a base – a rock-solid foundation. I am what I am because of hunting, specifically white-tailed deer hunting.

I was blessed to have been born to farm folks. My dad and grandfather operated a 500-acre potato farm in the heart of New York's famed Finger Lakes Region. My father, Charles H., was also a deer hunter who felt his only son needed to know what the deer woods were all about.

My journey as a deer hunter began long before I could ever legally carry a bow or firearm. In New York you cannot begin hunting deer with a firearm until you are 16, so from age five to 15 I tagged along at my dad's side or bird-dogged the local woodlots for other hunters. As I reflect back on those days I get goose bumps. They were great times to be young.

▶ The Five Stages of the Hunter

The heart and soul of the American deer hunter has been defined by researchers. Some twenty years ago *Deer & Deer Hunting* reported on a study done by Drs. Robert Jackson and Robert Norton from the LaCrosse campus of the University of Wisconsin. After interviewing over 1,000 deer hunters they concluded that America's deer hunters pass through five stages in their lifetime deer hunting journey. They are as follows:

The Shooter Stage: This is when the hunter begins. They need to have some success and be able to have a level of accomplishment.

The Limiting Out Stage: From stage one, most hunters progress to this stage. In stage two the hunter's goal is to harvest as many animals as is legally possible.

The Trophy Stage: In this stage, the hunter has enough knowledge of his quarry that he begins to exhibit selectivity in his hunt. Bigger antlers and a keen knowledge of stewarding the whitetail resource begin to take center stage in the deer hunter's life at this point.

The Method Stage: By the time a hunter reaches this stage he is beginning to mellow out. With many autumns under his belt he begins to become more interested in how he hunts. Understanding deer behavior also becomes paramount during this stage.

The Sportsman Stage: By the time a hunter hits this stage he truly knows who he is. He knows deer behavior, has killed many deer, has probably become involved in the preservation of hunting, and makes a conscious effort to see that hunting is passed on to the next generation. This is also the stage when many deer hunters become involved as managers of their own deer hunting properties. I've often viewed this stage as the reflective stage.

Though all five stages can stand alone, stages three through five can be and often are interwoven. As a 58-year-old I'm able to see this in my own life because I'm passionately interested in hunting mature bucks, learning all I can about whitetails, managing our farm's deer population, and sharing what I've learned with the public. Let me explain by sharing with you my five-stage experience.

In the early 1970s I was firmly immersed in the Shooter Stage. I was passionate about deer hunting and couldn't get enough of it.

►My Shooter Stage

Pinpointing when my Shooter Stage began is easy. Though I couldn't carry or shoot a gun it began when I was five years old, in the front seat of my dad's pickup truck. We were driving through our farm in mid-November when a big buck ran across the road in front of us, just missing the front of the truck. This occurred over 50 years ago, yet the sight of the mature buck bounding in front of us and across our harvested potato field is still etched in my mind. That event lit my whitetail fire – and it remains burning today.

When I was seven, my mom and dad got me a Daisy lever-action BB gun for Christmas. By the time I was 10 I had shot thousands of BBs through it, and I actually got pretty good with it. When I hit 12 I got my first real gun, a single-shot .22, for Christmas. What struck me was my new gun didn't go pop like the BB gun. It made a loud *bang!* I was hooked.

Well before my sixteenth birthday I'd gotten serious about woodchuck hunting. My hero was Jack O'Connor, *Outdoor Life's* Shooting Editor. I loved rifles so much that I had the Speer handloading manual nearly memorized.

In my early teens I graded potatoes for a local farmer on weekends during the winter months so I could earn the money to buy a .243. By the time I was 16 I was handloading my own ammunition in my bedroom, much to my mother's chagrin. Athletics and hunting were my focus and passion as a teen, and I did both every possible moment. No woodchuck on our farm was safe during my teenage years. Then when I could finally hunt deer, my passion for them took center stage.

►My Limiting Out Stage

As I reflect back this is probably the stage of my hunting life that I'm least proud of. With many hunters the Limiting Out Stage is a period when they feel that the only way they can prove their worth and prowess as a deer hunter is by how many deer they kill. This described me.

I had been putting in the time in the whitetail woods long before I could actually hunt deer so I knew a lot about deer behavior before I could hunt to kill. Consequently, I had a real jump start on other hunters my age. Because of this I tagged out early every year. The first buck I harvested, on my very first opening day, placed second in a local big buck contest. The next seven bucks were all yearlings. Though I would have loved to harvest a big-racked buck, any buck was okay in my early years. My goal was to prove I could do it, and do it ASAP.

In 1974 New York's permit system allowed for a two buck limit. In those days I wouldn't think of passing on a buck and actually harvested both of these bucks on the same day. I had both feet firmly entrenched in the Limiting Out Stage.

It took me a while to fall in love with bow hunting. By 1979, when I harvested my first good bow buck, I was creeping closer and closer to the Trophy Stage.

By the mid-1980s I was looking at deer hunting much differently. I was passing bucks and working hard to master methods. The Method Stage had won me over.

In the late 1980s I began to think about all aspects of deer hunting, from stewarding the land to hunting better deer. This is the first mature buck I rattled in and harvested on our farm. It was a great day.

Fortunately, I didn't spend too much time in this stage before coming to my senses.

Much of my progression from this stage to the next came about because of the 35mm camera. I returned from Vietnam on December 3, 1970, and was discharged from the U.S. Air Force that day. While in Vietnam I purchased a 35mm camera and a long telephoto lens. I had become fascinated by Erwin Bauer's and Lenny Rue's whitetail photography and was challenged to see if I could get images that rivaled theirs. So, in the winter of 1971 my journey as a whitetail photographer began while attending college. The camera changed my life forever. It also changed me as a hunter.

▶My Trophy Stage

By my twenty-sixth birthday I had graduated from college and married. The Trophy Stage of my hunting journey began to manifest itself. The athlete in me still drove me to limit out but I started to look at deer hunting differently. I knew how much smarter mature bucks were than the yearlings I'd been regularly harvesting and the challenge they presented started to shift my focus toward hunting older, smarter bucks. I began spending the entire year scouting and photographing whitetails, learning all I could about their behavior. My true education as a whitetail photographer and hunter began in this stage.

In my late twenties I began lecturing and along with it came writing assignments for the Stump Sitters, the forerunner of *Deer & Deer Hunting* magazine. It didn't take me long to envision that I might be able to make a career out of writing, photographing and hunting the whitetail.

Probably the trophy stage is mischaracterized more than any other stage the hunter goes through. Many think of it as the period of time when the lure of big antlers obscures the true reason for hunting. This assessment is unfortunate. In my case the trophy stage solidified my love for hunting and helped me understand why a man would sit for long hours in rain, sleet and snow to hunt a four-legged animal with bone on his head. For non-hunters the thought of this is bizarre.

This stage taught me more about the rhythms of nature than any other because I was spending far more time in the woods, learning about all aspects of nature. No longer was I in a hurry to limit out. I was beginning to see the bigger picture of why some men become passionate about the white-tailed deer.

Due to the time I was spending observing, photographing and hunting whitetails the spoils of these efforts began to come along. Though it was very difficult I found that it was possible to

In 1989 I took my first out-of-country hunt, to Anticosti Island. Though the deer weren't what I expected, the experience was an eye-opener.

Passing up younger bucks and learning all I could about whitetails has enriched my hunting experience beyond measure.

As I inched past age 50 I became passionate about land management and raising better deer. I was firmly immersed in the Sportsman's Stage.

hunt and harvest older class bucks through patience, perseverance and being a keen observer of deer behavior.

I make no apologies about my passion for this stage. It made me a far better hunter and conservationist than I ever would have been if I had continued to stay in the first two stages. To me there is nothing wrong with this stage. Nearly every mature buck hunter I know shoots three times as many does as bucks and many go multiple years between harvesting bucks. In the process a true trophy stage hunter is immersed in thoughts of why he hunts and the methods he uses to pursue the whitetail.

▶My Method Stage

If I had been involved in the research I would have thought the Method Stage would come before the Trophy Stage. Actually for me it is tough to differentiate between these stages. To get into the Trophy Stage I had to know and understand the Method Stage. Though I'm firmly entrenched in the Method Stage, the two preceding stages are still very much present in my life and career.

For as long as I can remember I've been fascinated with whitetail behavior. This caused me to finally build my own white-tailed deer research facility here on our farm in 1995. The facility's 35-acre enclosure, coupled with the farm's remaining 165 acres of quality deer management land has provided me with the ultimate behavior research location. The enclosure's 15 whitetails (which are not hunted) and the free-ranging deer on the balance of the farm (which are hunted) offer a unique window to the whitetail's world.

Living with whitetails every day of the year has helped to refine how I pursue them with bow, gun and camera. Some of the techniques I've incorporated

The benefits of the Sportsman's Stage have allowed a window into the whitetail's world I never thought possible. When I harvested this buck on our farm in 1996, I realized that all the hard work was paying off.

into my hunting have caused some raised eyebrows over the years – from both biologists and armchair hunters. However, none of the strategies I use and write about are pipe dreams or hocus-pocus. They've all come about through years of constant observation and trial and error.

▶ My Sportsman's Stage

At some point many hunters reach a place where they feel they've seen it all, done it all. For a few there are more mountains to climb, providing their fire is still lit. For those with a passion for whitetails and deer hunting, the Sportsman's Stage is a period in a hunter's life when he reflects on where he has been and wonders what is left in his tank. If he is willing and able, the Sportsman's Stage can be very fulfilling.

In many ways I entered this stage in December of 1989, when I met legendary deer biologist Al Brothers while photographing on the Jambers' Ranch in South Texas. This encounter really got me thinking about what I call *Total Deer Management*,

I'm blessed. I've lived all five stages of the hunter's journey and still feel passionate about what I do. It's been an incredible journey.

the management of all segments of the deer population as well as the natural habitat and all the wildlife that inhabit the property. Many now look at TDM as quality deer management.

Since 1989 I've become immersed in practicing TDM/QDM on our farm. Many other local landowners have embraced it as well. Consequently, what has occurred here in western New York has been impressive. Though I always spent a lot of time scouting, planting food plots and photographing deer, the whole concept of Total Deer Management has been a real eye-opener. Not only has it made me a better hunter but I've become more knowledgeable of whitetail behavior. The process has spilled over, resulting in a better understanding of our farm's entire ecosystem.

My Sportsman's Stage also gave me the opportunity to have a greater bond with my son, Aaron. He was just learning to hunt in the early 1990s, and our deer management/hunting journey has proven to be very special. The bottom line to all of this is that my Sportsman's Stage, with a lot of the Trophy and Method Stages thrown in, has been a blessing from God.

Not long ago my friend Joe Hamilton wrote an article for *Quality Whitetails* titled *A Hunter's Path*. In many ways it was a reflective piece. His ending words touched me and are worth sharing.

"This is my creed. A seasoned hunter, one with the hunting spirit, pursues his quarry on each occasion with the enthusiasm of his first encounter and with the reverence as though it were his last. I, for one, do not want to know when I have had my last hunt.

"How do I wish to be remembered? Simply this: In his chest beat the heart of a hunter – a seasoned hunter who embraced the spirit of the hunt as he lived and how he lived so that those who follow will have a secure and well-defined path."

Joe's words pretty much sum up why I do what I do. I've been blessed to have lived in America, doing what I consider to be the greatest job on Earth. In the process the white-tailed deer has given me a quality of life like none other.

I feel very fortunate to have lived long enough to experience all five stages of the hunter. It's been a special journey – one scripted in Heaven.

CHAPTER 17

More Than an Animal to Me

What does the whitetail mean to you? Have you ever thought what your life would be like if it wasn't part of your life? Chances are that America's favorite deer evokes a million different feelings within hunters across this great land. The whitetail has a way of being both an inspiration and an addiction at the same time. Why else would anyone sit in a tree stand for hours in the most miserable conditions known to man? Through rain, sleet, and snow, deer hunters keep coming back for more.

I'd hate to think what my life would have been like without the whitetail. It was what truly introduced me to nature. As a little kid the graceful figure of a mature buck running across a plowed field on our farm was what lit my fire, a fire that has kept me heading back to the woods for nearly 50 years.

In my wildest dreams I never envisioned having a career in the outdoor field. You see, I've gone through a process of sorts in my relationship with the whitetail. When I was a young boy all I wanted to do was get a glimpse of them. Then, during my teenage years, the thrill of hunting whitetails was a big part of my life. As I climbed the hill of life I went from being a young man to a middle-aged one. In the process, the way I looked at life

In the 1980s I became a field editor for *Deer & Deer Hunting* magazine. Shortly afterward, I traveled to Wisconsin for a deer hunt with the magazine's other staff. An incredible journey had begun.

and the things around me changed. The thrill of the hunt took on a new dimension – the desire to know all I could about whitetails.

The "desire to know" became much more important than the dos and don'ts of hunting deer. The more I learned, the more I kept coming back to one thought: the whitetail wasn't just an animal made up of X amount of skin, bones and antlers. To me, it's far more than merely an animal.

▶ Reflection

Last summer I was patrolling and scouting our farm. The late summer day had been rather cool and clear. The sun was dropping below the tree line as I rounded the corner of a spruce plantation on the north end of the farm. Fifty yards ahead my eyes caught movement in the golden rods. I came to a stop and turned off the Gator just as a doe and two fawns stepped into the roadway. For the next couple minutes they surveyed me before bounding off.

Rather than firing up the engine and continuing on I chose to sit back and listen to the sounds of nature. To me the chorus made by insects at nightfall is one of the greatest songs on earth.

In the Eastern sky the moon slowly crested the horizon. As daylight vanished I sat in awe. Time flew by and before I knew it the rising moon had turned into my street light. As I reached for the key to start the engine I couldn't help but think of how blessed I was. I also realized that the blessing I'd just experienced was a direct result of my encounter with the three whitetails. As I pulled away from the goldenrod field and headed home my mind was full of the thoughts of life.

During the hundreds of hours I've huddled behind a camera and sat in a deer stand I've come to realize that the whitetail is far more than an animal. To me the experiences and relationships it has brought my way have been far more rewarding than things crafted by man's hands.

The white-tailed deer brought Paul Daniels and Terry Rice into my life. The bond and friendship we've built over the years has been very special.

In 1989 I traveled to Texas where I met George Jambers and Al Brothers. Their approach to land and deer management changed my perspective of whitetail management when they introduced me to quality deer management.

▶ The People

Had it not been for the human relationships the whitetail has brought my way, it's doubtful whether my life would be as fulfilled as it's been. It's because of the whitetail that I've come to know the likes of Paul Daniels, Terry Rice, George Jambers, Ben Lingle, Bob Avery, Dave Buckley, Craig Dougherty, Bentley Brown, Dave Oathout, Don Haingray and the many great editors of *Deer and Deer Hunting* magazine. All of these men have played a huge part in making my career what it is.

To do the things I do with a camera often requires involvement from others, and Paul Daniels and Terry Rice have been like brothers to me – brothers I never had growing up. Both are great deer hunters and two of the best photo models a hunting and whitetail photographer could ever hope to have. Paul, in particular, has been close. We've hunted, traveled and literally wept together. It's been one of those special life-long relationships made possible because of the whitetail.

George Jambers, Bob Avery and Ben Lingle are special human beings. Jambers and Avery are now gone but all three, aside from being successful businessmen,

The whitetail was responsible for my meeting and becoming friends with two of the most incredible whitetail experts in the business, Dave Buckley and Dave Oathout.

were serious deer hunters who worked hard to raise the best whitetails possible on their property. They also opened their heart and property to me. In all cases they had no clue who I was when we met, just that I admired the whitetail as much as they did. In each case a special bond formed and over the years all let me photograph to my heart's content on their property, when others were not allowed access. For this I feel most fortunate. But more importantly the wonderful times we shared on their respective properties have enriched my life beyond measure.

And then there are the *Deer and Deer Hunting* editors I've worked with for over 25 years. Though all had and have their own unique style of doing things each became a special part of my life. Al Hofacker, Jack Brauer, Pat Durkin and Dan Schmidt have been guiding lights in the incredible career I've forged. I'd hate to think how my life would have turned out had they not been there to mold and shape me. One thing is certain, had it not been for the white-tailed deer, our paths never would have crossed.

▶ Chance Encounter

From time to time I'll have people come up to me

at speaking engagements and discuss different things. Often I'm asked about articles I've written. This may come as a surprise, but the two most-remembered magazine articles I've penned were not how-tos on hunting. They were "The Journey" (an article about my son and me) and "One Man's Battle with Lyme Disease," which I did for *Deer and Deer Hunting.* I feel fortunate to have written both but in terms of impacting humanity the latter (a story about my encounter with Lyme disease) is probably the most meaningful piece I've ever written. Here's why.

About 10 years ago I traveled to Warren, Pennsylvania, to do a deer hunting seminar. Prior to the show I was sitting at my book table signing things and a man in his thirties came up to the table. Our eyes locked and I could see his lips beginning to tremble. I also noticed his eyes watering. For a split second I wasn't sure what was going on. The person then attempted to talk. His voice broke and he managed to say, "I'm sorry."

He paused, regained his composure then said, with tears running down his cheeks, "I want to thank you for saving my life." I was stunned – I didn't know what to say.

I've hunted with many whitetail outfitters. The best, by a wide margin, is Saskatchewan's Bentley Brown. He's a great whitetail outfitter and an even better person. There is no way our paths would have crossed had it not been for whitetails.

I remember asking, "What do you mean?" The guy went on to say that for the better part of two years he found his life slipping away from him. No matter how many doctors he went to see none could find out why his health was deteriorating. Then he read my article on Lyme disease. Ironically the symptoms I encountered were similar to his. He got in contact with Dr. Joseph Joseph, who treated my Lyme, and discovered that he, too, had Lyme disease. He began treatment for Lyme and from the brink of disaster his life was turned around.

So, there I was, in Warren, Pennsylvania,

I've seen many hunting camps in my 40+ years of pursuing whitetails but none better than Craig Dougherty's Kindred Spirits. I've learned more about life than whitetails during my time there.

While conducting a deer hunting seminar in Warren, Pennsylvania, I discovered how one of my non-hunting articles helped a fellow hunter.

experiencing one of the most rewarding times of my life. My association with the whitetail had allowed for a new and different twist to life's journey – that of helping a fellow man. Since this experience I've been amazed by the number of people this particular article has helped. There wasn't a sentence in the article telling how to become a better deer hunter. But what the piece did was help a lot of hunters (and non-hunters) regain the gift of life and that's far more important than anything I could ever write about.

▶The Experience

I'll never forget the time I was standing beside a waterfall in a nearby state park. The day was beautiful and the scene was breathtaking. While watching the water cascade down the falls I noticed a family of four approaching. As they walked by I overheard the teenage boy say to his mom, "This is boring, when are we going home?" His words nearly blew my mind. My guess is that the kid would have preferred being home on his computer instead of experiencing nature. I felt like telling the boy

This Adirondack whitetail, named Charlie by the landowner, helped launch my whitetail career. The relationship we had was beyond belief.

that it doesn't get any better than this.

In retrospect the whitetail introduced me to nature. It's because of the lure of the whitetail that I came to love and appreciate everything from wildflowers, to sunsets, to raging rivers and mountains. In my case everything fed off of what I admired most about the whitetail. During the course of the journey I fell in love with photographing all aspects of nature. I'm best known for the photographic images I've made of the whitetail but photographing a beautiful sunset or a carpet of wildflowers gets my inner juices flowing just as fast as photographing a big whitetail buck. Photography has caused my natural roots to run deep into this country's soil.

But I don't have to be gripping a camera, gun or bow to be energized by the whitetail's world. My forays into the whitetail's woods have caused some special bonds with the real estate I've walked. Some of the ridges, swamps and stands of oaks have left a lasting impression on me. Our farm is a prime example. Though only 200 acres, there are several locations where memories have been etched from years of going back to the same spots to hunt.

In the Northwest corner of the farm is a huge beech tree in the center of a 10-acre stand of 100+ year-old oak trees. It's here that I can witness the grandeur of a sunrise and sunset from the same homemade, permanent tree stand. Though there may be better deer stands on the property I still go back to the blind because of the memories I've formed over the years. Whenever I sit in it and scan the wood's different trees and shooting lanes I'm reminded of different times and experiences. In many ways the old stand is an archive of my lifetime of deer hunting.

►The Animal

Over the last 25 years I've been blessed to have photographed wildlife from the Everglades to Alaska. Through these experiences I've come to realize that no other animal can stack up to the whitetail when beauty, grace and compatibility with man are factored in. It is simply in a class by itself.

The key to much of the whitetail behavior I've been able to photograph over the years came to me by accident. While photographing on a large estate in the fall of 1986, I discovered a side of whitetails that has enabled me to truly get "up close and personal" with certain deer.

One day while baiting around my photo blind I discovered a button buck staring at me from 30 yards away. Our eyes locked and I figured he'd run at any moment. When he didn't, I tossed him some corn to see what he'd do. Well, to make a long story short, I was able to get this buck and several other deer to imprint on the sound of shelled corn rattling around in a plastic can. The amazing thing is that by shaking the can I was able to get these deer to tolerate my presence.

Interestingly that button buck lived to be nine and a half years old. Over those years he allowed me to follow him in his wanderings, provided I had the food. In the end he wasn't a majestic-looking buck, but he wore the scars of his nine years well. He eluded predators, endured incredible buck fights, and survived the brutal northern winters before dying of what appeared to be natural causes. Rather than let coyotes consume his body I buried him beside a small stream, not unlike the small stream where we had met on a cool autumn day nine years before. Though it

seems like a fairy tale, he and I formed a bond that's a true love story, one that will probably never be repeated in nature.

Since 1986 I have used the same imprinting technique on an estate in Pennsylvania, deer wintering areas in New York's Adirondack Mountains, a ranch in Texas, and other locations. Actually the principle is nothing new; Pavlov was the first to study a conditioned response from animals. Over the last 15 years this technique has provided me a window into the whitetail's world few humans have ever seen. Lest you think I have some mysterious power over whitetails, let me set the record straight: I've encountered many people from around the country who have also been able to get wild deer to imprint on foods and different sounds associated with it. So, what I've done is not new or unique, it's just that few people have discovered it. So, "now you know the rest of the story." Well, not quite.

There's no question that this discovery, break, fluke, or whatever you want to call it has enabled me to have a special relationship with the whitetail that even researchers haven't had. People often ask me

Of all my accomplishments as a hunter and photographer none has been greater than the experience of introducing my son Aaron to hunting. The times we've spent in the deer woods have been precious.

how I've been able to record the different behaviors in whitetails that almost no one else has seen. Well, it's because of that button buck in 1986, a buck that the landowner came to call "Charlie."

Charlie allowed me a window into the whitetail's world that may never be repeated. When I think of his tolerance of me I think of one thing – disbelief. In the physical realm Charlie was 100% white-tailed deer but hopefully you will not mind if I submit to you that he truly thought he was part human – or that he thought I was part deer. I'll let you decide. Regardless, the eight-plus years we knew each other was one of those "believe it or not" relationships which is hard to believe unless it was witnessed.

▶ Blood Ties

In the 1970s I was immersed in a corporate sales and marketing career. My turf was the hallways of government and some of the biggest corporations in America. It was an exciting time in my life. Then something happened. In 1977 my wife Carla and I had our only child, a son we named Aaron, and my life was changed forever.

Up to that point I hunted as much as I could but was never able to find enough time to do it. When Aaron was just shy of two years old I decided to make a career change (with the blessing of Carla) and go full-time into outdoor writing and photography. Part of this decision was to be able to spend more time with Aaron. On September 1, 1979, I walked out of corporate America and into the American wilderness.

Carla was a public school teacher, so when I left the corporate world we had to decide what to do with Aaron when I was traveling and photographing. Rather than place him with a baby sitter I took him with me—everywhere. To understand where I'm coming from envision a 6′2″ guy with a big camera slung over one shoulder and a two-year-old boy over the other shoulder. That was me. I'll be the first to admit that there were some very awkward times, but I wouldn't trade the times or the memories for anything. Aaron went with me wherever I went,

whether it was to check traplines, to speaking engagements, to deer stands, to the Everglades, to the Rockies or Alaska. Simply put, Aaron didn't fit the mold of the average kid growing up in America.

Because most of our time was spent in the whitetail's world he and I learned many things about deer together. I'll never forget the first time I used a commercial deer call in 1985. They had just come out and I was anxious to see how they worked. Well, we found out how good they were.

Huddled in a tightly woven ground blind I had made on our farm, I grunted two bucks to within 15 yards of our stand, late one afternoon. There I was with the tube in my mouth "talking to the bucks" and Aaron whispering in my ear, "Daddy, are you going to shoot them?" Well, I didn't. I chose to pass on both because of their size. As I reflect on the experience I still get goose bumps. The value of that moment in my life's memory chest is priceless.

The effect of the whitetail on both our lives has been cumulative. It gave both of us a greater appreciation for nature and the great God we serve. The bottom line is that the whitetail has truly been the linchpin that has allowed our relationship to grow and blossom over the years.

▶ Gold At the End of the Rainbow

I sometimes wonder about people's values. There's a popular bumper sticker that reads, "He who dies with the most toys wins." Sadly too many in America are swept up by this mentality. Gadgets, toys, bricks and mortar are nothing more than things. Personally I think Swindoll's quote has more meaning. "The greatest things in life are not things – the greatest things in life are experiences and relationships." And many of the special relationships I've had in my life are a direct result of my association with the white-tailed deer. In many ways I've struck gold.

If I were to die tomorrow I'd have no regrets. Thanks to God and one of his creatures – the whitetail – I've been blessed beyond measure. A man can't ask for any more.

By the time Aaron was six he was accompanying me on many of my hunts.

When Aaron was nine we shared a successful bowhunt together. Besides imparting hunting knowledge at such times, I used these opportunities to teach deer anatomy and biology.

were my sanctuary. I knew the hummocks, gullies and ravines as if they were extensions of my bedroom.

But my life's journey made a drastic turn when I was 12. My parents split, and my dad went into the construction business 70 miles away. Our hunting time dwindled and I didn't see much of him at a critical point in my life. For nearly four years I stopped hunting and immersed myself in athletics. Then, at the urging of a friend, I became interested in hunting again when I was 16. That four-year absence proved positive. It made me realize how much I missed hunting and the woods.

▶ Early Adulthood

This appreciation was magnified in 1969 and 1970 when I spent 14 months in Vietnam with the U.S. Air Force. Many negative things have been written about Vietnam. But war's horrors gave me a reference point, providing a positive influence on my life. War made me appreciate America and all it stands for.

"Life, liberty and the pursuit of happiness" took on new meaning after I came home in 1970. My dad and I became closer than we had been in years, and we hunted deer together for the first time in nearly a decade. The smells and sights of the woods helped

rekindle the bond we knew when I was a youngster.

I also came home with a new companion, the 35mm camera. I was introduced to these cameras in Vietnam, and I desired to hunt whitetails with them. The more I photographed whitetails, the more I wanted to be in the woods. The true journey had just begun.

In 1973 my wife, Carla, and I bought our farm which bordered the farm I had grown up on. We turned it into a wildlife sanctuary. Then, after five years of marriage, God blessed us with our only child, a son. Once Aaron was old enough to sit up and crawl I took him everywhere. If I went scouting on a warm summer evening, he went along. If I went someplace to photograph deer, he went along. At times he was noisy in the woods but I didn't care. We were learning together. Those times together often caused me to reflect. My childhood flashed in front of me. I saw my dad and myself back on the farm.

When Aaron was nearly two, Carla returned to teaching, and I resigned my position in corporate sales and marketing to pursue a full-time career in the outdoors. Rather than hire a baby-sitter, we decided Aaron would spend the days with me.

Needless to say, we had some interesting times.

▶A New Direction

As a traveling lecturer, photographer and writer, I saw America changing rapidly in its views toward hunting. I was concerned and wanted to do something about it. The pen can be powerful, but I learned early there is only so much you can do to influence people about hunting. For me, hunting is more than words. It's amber sunrises and the smell of leaves in an October forest. It's fluffy snow flakes landing on a cold gun barrel, and the smell of wet wool at the end of a day's hunt. It's the rapid heartbeat as a white-tailed buck gracefully moves through the woods, and the "fummmp" sound of an arrow's release. It's the skinning, butchering and cooking process of getting the deer from the woods to the table.

In short, hunting is being there. It's experiencing all that nature offers.

It was these things and more that I wanted Aaron to see and experience. Hunting and nature had given me so much, and I wanted him to understand and experience all of it. I'm sure we must have looked like a peculiar pair, a guy with a big camera and his little kid moving through the woods. After stopping to photograph a scenic setting, I often found Aaron picking flowers for his mom. On other occasions we would just sit in the woods, and he would ask me all kinds of questions about leaves, birds and trees. In a way, Aaron wasn't introduced to nature; he was born into it.

The finality of hunting came for him at age four. I came home to get him before I gutted and dragged a buck out of the woods. I'll never forget his words upon seeing the downed deer: "Daddy, is the deer sleeping? Why doesn't he get up?"

Aaron had seen deer hanging in the barn, but the scene was far different from seeing one lying in the woods. I slowly and patiently explained that I had killed it for us to eat.

He said, "You mean this is what they look like before we eat supper?"

I chuckled and explained to him what went into getting a deer from the woods to the supper table. As

Aaron, at age 11 in 1988, helps me drag out a buck.

I took my knife from its sheath, he said, "Can I watch you take its insides out?"

"Of course," I said, and we squatted beside the buck. Even though Aaron was only four, this first biology class was fascinating for him, and for me. He wanted to know about the various organs, and I carefully dissected the heart to show him what it looked like. Once done, he helped me drag the deer out of the woods.

In those days we butchered our own deer, and Aaron wanted to be in on the process. One of his tasks was to carry the meat from the cutting table to the grinder. Carla then let him cut some of the tape to seal the packages for freezing. It was a family affair, from the woods to the freezer. After that, Aaron wanted to help with all the deer I killed.

▶Hunter/Trapper

Besides deer hunting, I also trapped fox, raccoon

After 12 years of tagging along with me, Aaron began his hunting career at age 14.

On a cool crisp day in October Aaron killed his first whitetail, a doe, with his bow. He was 15 at the time.
In contrast, I was 30 when I killed my first deer with a bow.

By the time Aaron was 16 he had become a very good bow hunter.

and I climbed to the summit of Mount Washburn. Along the way we photographed a big bull moose that was bedded near the hiking trail.

Once at the top, we sat and gazed for 100 miles in every direction. When a band of bighorn sheep grazed past us 30 yards away, I started taking pictures. As the camera's motor drive hummed, Aaron whispered, "Dad, didn't God make us a beautiful world?" It was enough to melt my heart. It made me realize that adults need to slow down to see nature through the eyes of a child, and appreciate what God has given us. That trip didn't involve hunting, but it laid the groundwork for Aaron's appreciation of nature, and set the stage for his understanding of stewardship. Though I was trying to teach him, I began realizing he was also teaching me. Since then, our trips throughout North America have solidified our deep love for nature.

When Aaron turned six, I started taking him hunting. I began slowly at first, knowing all too well that staying quiet and motionless is difficult for a youngster. I picked situations where we would not be sitting long. He would get off the school bus, and we would often head to a favorite ground blind to sit the last hour of the day.

When he was seven, he was with me when I killed a white-tailed doe. We watched the deer more than 30 minutes before I clicked off the shotgun's safety and fired.

I viewed taking him with me on photo trips, lectures and backyard hunting sits as "seed" time. My goal was to make each trip a positive experience. I made it a point not to push guns and bows on Aaron. I was a baseball coach for 25 years, and saw too many parents push their favorite sport on their children. I knew how much he loved nature, and how he always wanted to go with me. But I didn't know if he would like to hunt and actually kill an animal. If he didn't want to, I was prepared to live with his choice.

When he was nine, Aaron asked if we could shoot the .22 rifle. When he was 10, he wanted to start shooting a bow. That Christmas he got his first bow and he began shooting in our basement. Since then he's been involved in much of what I do, from

and muskrats on the farm. Before Aaron started kindergarten, he and I had a ritual during trapping season. Each morning after breakfast we headed for the Back 40 to check my trap line. It was during the trapping sessions that he learned much about nature's balance. We would often discuss why animal populations must be kept in check. That would occasionally be reinforced when I found a mangy fox in a trap. It allowed him to see firsthand that nature's way of killing is often cruel and prolonged. I would use these times to illustrate the importance of trapping and hunting.

When Aaron was 4-1/2, we went to the Rocky Mountains on a working vacation. After speaking for a week at a camp in Jackson Hole, Wyoming, we headed for Yellowstone National Park. One afternoon, Aaron

As the years passed Aaron become a very good deer hunter, as evidenced by his 1998 buck.

By the time 2000 rolled around Aaron was an integral part of our deer management program. We've become a fine-tuned father and son team.

modeling for hunting photos to helping with the farm's habitat work. In many ways our life has been a script written in Heaven.

Heavy Stuff

In 1992, Aaron was a finalist in his high school's public speaking contest. When he began preparing for it I asked what his speech was on. He said, "The Animal Rights Myth."

"Why'd you pick that topic?" I asked.

"Because I want to share the positive side of the issue. All anyone ever hears is the negative side of hunting, and I want to share my perspective."

I looked at him and thought. "Wow, that's pretty heady stuff for a high school freshman."

I went to the contest not knowing what his chances would be. He was going up against experienced seniors, so I knew winning would be difficult. Well, Aaron didn't win, a senior did, but as I sat watching him address the entire school I thought to myself: "Man, he's articulating things better than most adults could ever hope to do. Today, hunting is a big winner."

As I reflect on hunting in America, I think of our country's youth. Unfortunately, too many parents don't have the time or desire to share the outdoors with their kids. There is a familiar quote that says, "We have filled our lives with meaningless trophies." Sadly, that sums up America too well.

For many, the quest for more gadgets, gizmos, money and positions has caused family and traditions to be cast aside. Unfortunately, parents baby sit their kids with TV, Nintendo and computerized junk instead of showing them what the outdoors is all about. In other cases, kids with loving but single parents can only dream of what might have been. I know the latter all too well.

A New Chapter

It was Sunday, October 22, a great day in western New York. It dawned clear and cold, the kind of day every bowhunter dreams of seeing. After going to church with Carla and Aaron, we celebrated his birthday. It seemed hard to believe that he was now a man in his twenties. From the time I woke up my mind drifted to the memories we had shared since he came into the world. I couldn't help but wonder where the years had gone. In a little over 20 short years he had gone from being a little tyke, following me around in the woods, to becoming a 6´3″ giant of a man involved in the corporate world.

After an early afternoon dinner Aaron said: "What do you say we end the day in a deer stand." Because of what he is now doing this would be the first time we would hunt together in a long time, so I jumped at

On opening day 2002 Aaron killed his best buck to date. A day later I harvested the best buck to come from our farm. It was a year to remember.

the opportunity. A couple hours before sundown we headed to our favorite haunts on our farm. The temperature had risen to 60 degrees so I didn't expect much action, but even so, just the thought of our hunting together and seeing a sunset from a deer stand would be more than enough.

The first hour was slow, with only a few squirrels scurrying around in the woods. Then, with about

an hour of daylight left, a doe and two fawns passed under my stand before entering a nearby food plot. Within minutes a 2-1/2-year-old eight-pointer slipped through the hardwoods and into the plot. During the next 45 minutes three yearling bucks appeared to fill their bellies, along with 19 turkeys. It was quite a sight to see the bucks, does and turkeys feeding in the same field.

Three generations of Alsheimer deer hunters. Aaron, my dad Charles H. and I enjoyed some wonderful days in the woods together.

With no interest in killing any of the bucks, I studied the turkeys through my binoculars as they fed off in Aaron's direction. Above crisscrossing jet trails and cirrus clouds began turning amber as the sun inched toward the horizon. With no air movement whatever I could actually hear a doe munching on clover as legal shooting time ended. I slipped my arrow into the bow's quiver and sat motionless for several minutes before climbing from the stand. I wanted to treasure the scene as long as I could.

After gathering up my equipment I began crossing the food plot to pick up Aaron. He was at the base of his tree waiting for me. When I got to him I whispered: "What did you see?"

He responded. "Boy, what a day. That was a great sit."

"Well, what did you see?" I repeated.

He countered: "Oh, just a couple does, 19 turkeys and a great sunset."

"No bucks?" I said.

In one motion he swung his arm around my neck and shoulder and hugged me before saying, "No, just God's handiwork. That and a chance to hunt again with you is more than enough."

I was speechless; my eyes began to water as I stared into his eyes from two feet away. His affection and words tugged at my heart. It was a special moment for me – one part elation, one part sadness all rolled into one. Throughout early fall I had been thinking about what it was like to hunt alone after so many years of having Aaron in the woods with me.

In many ways the readers of *Deer and Deer Hunting* magazine have seen Aaron grow up with me. He's not only been a great model for my photos but also a hunting companion and someone I've been able to learn many things from. So, he's been far more than a great son. To say we have an incredible father/son relationship would be a vast understatement.

▶ A Lesson from the Past

Early in my career I hunted a deer camp in the heart of Pennsylvania called Camp Harmony. The purpose for going there was to get a glimpse of what camp hunting was like and share the experience with the readers of *Deer and Deer Hunting*.

Camp Harmony was a special place, very rustic, but more than adequate and in many ways comfortable beyond measure. I'll never forget seeing it for the first time as Dick Snavely and I wound our way down a narrow forested road, in the heart of Pennsylvania Game Lands. The setting reminded me of a painting I had once seen.

In retrospect I didn't appreciate the experience as much as I should have. I should have paid more attention to the give and take and love shown between the camp's fathers and their grown sons rather than being so focused on the deer hunting. While I was out in the woods checking for deer sign they were back at camp sharing a lifetime of memories.

At the time my son was very young so I wasn't able to see far enough into my future to realize that the day would come when I'd be where Camp Harmony's fathers were in their relationships with their sons. Now, as I reflect I can see that the beauty of Camp Harmony wasn't the deer, but rather, the father/son bond and the love I witnessed during my brief stay there.

Unfortunately, it took me a long time to figure out that there is a bigger reason for deer hunting than the kill. As I reflect on the part hunting has played in my life I now understand how special the relationships that I've forged with my son and friends have been. Relationships and experiences trump things every time.

▶ Gifts of Time

On my office wall is a sign with the following quote: "In the eyes of a child, love is spelled TIME."

My father gave me the time when I was his "little shaver," and I learned from his gift. As a result, I made time for Aaron. When I think of the memories my son and I have shared, my eyes well with tears. It's the greatest investment I ever made, and the dividends have been worth more than silver or gold.

The other day I took the long way to town, over the hill and past the farm where my life began. I pulled off the road at the top of the hill, got out of my van, and walked off the road to get a better view.

The sight from the hilltop was just as I remembered it. Stretching before me was a sea of farm fields gouged here and there with tree-choked ravines. In the distance my boyhood farmhouse stood out like an island. Through the bright sunlight I focused on the long hedgerow behind the house. It still looked as I remembered it. There are loads of memories in that slice of brush.

Even though more than 45 seasons have come and gone, it seemed like only yesterday that I was testing my hunting skill on the woodchucks that called it home. It was there that my love for hunting was born when a potato farmer and his son found time to be together with a single-shot .22 rifle.

▶ Conclusion

The longer I live, the more I realize the brevity of life's journey. Winston Churchill was so right when he said: "We make a living by what we get, but we make a life by what we give."

The most important thing for hunting is not whether record whitetails fall. It's ensuring future generations can experience the world's greatest outdoor experience: hunting whitetails on crisp autumn mornings. That's a journey that requires an investment of time, but it's worth the trip. I know. I've been there. And I try every day to appreciate the journey because none of us knows how long it will last.

As you head to the deer woods this fall, take time to reflect on family, relationships and the memories formed from past deer hunts. This is what matters most.

Index

A

Aaron, 7, 134, 169, 178-179, 181-190
Adirondack Mountains, 81, 178
Adult-doe-to-antlered-buck ratio, 55, 81, 131, 134
Aggression, 34, 44, 93, 97
Aggressive-snort, 94-95
Alabama, 86
Alkalinity, 150
Ambush, 62-63, 65, 71, 89, 92, 105, 142
Antler mass, 116
Antler pedicel, 55
Antlers, 24-25, 31, 35, 46, 55, 80, 93, 95-97, 106-107, 109-111, 113-116, 126, 152, 162, 165, 172
ATVs, 135
Auditory canal, 16
Autofocus, 122
Autumnal equinox, 80-84, 86-87
Avery, Bob, 173

B

Baiting, 84-85, 124-125, 178
Barometer, 34, 50, 77
Barometric pressure, 50, 54, 56, 77
Basic grunt, 94
Basket racks, 110
Bauer, Erwin, 165
Bedding areas, 64, 71, 102, 146
Bedding, 46, 57, 63-65, 71-73, 81, 89-92, 102, 105-107, 141, 146-147
Benches, 63
Bernier, Dick, 7, 85
Biggs, Mike, 120
Bird-dog trot, 42-43
Bleat, 93-94, 105-106
Bleats, 34, 76, 93
Body language, 26, 34
Boone and Crockett, 110, 112, 116
Boundary, 61, 90
Brassica, 151-152, 157
Brauer, Jack, 3, 7, 174
Breath, 6, 42, 75, 115
Breeding phase, 24-25, 35-36, 39, 87, 89, 105-106
Breeding window, 87
Breeding, 20, 24-25, 29, 31-32, 34-36, 39-43, 45-46, 55-56, 69, 81-84, 87, 89-90, 95-96, 99, 101-102, 105-106
Breeding, 20, 24-25, 29, 31-32, 34-36, 39-43, 45-46, 55-56, 69, 81-84, 87, 89-90, 95-96, 99, 101-102, 105-106

Breeding, 20, 24-25, 29, 31-32, 34-36, 39-43, 45-46, 55-56, 69, 81-84, 87, 89-90, 95-96, 99, 101-102, 105-106
Brothers, Al, 140, 168, 173
Brown, Bentley, 173, 175
Browse, 113, 140, 144, 146
Brush, 12, 44-46, 63, 65, 86, 113, 140, 144, 190
Buckley, Dave, 173-174
BushHawk, 123

C

Calling, 33, 74, 76, 92-93, 105-106, 133
Calling, 33, 74, 76, 92-93, 105-106, 133
Camera, 6, 8, 11, 21, 93-94, 119, 121-123, 125-126, 165, 167, 172-173, 177, 179, 183-184, 186
Canada, 113
Charlie, 6-7, 177, 179
Chase phase, 35, 39, 85
Chasing, 19, 24-25, 29, 32, 35-36, 39-41, 53, 55, 80-85, 87, 90, 94, 101, 106, 134
Chicory, 151-152, 156
Chlorophyll, 75
Chronic Wasting Disease, 125
Clover, 71-72, 107, 151-153, 156-157, 189
Cloverleaf, 107
Corn, 57, 71, 102-103, 125, 154-155, 178
Corn, 57, 71, 102-103, 125, 154-155, 178
Crab Orchard National Wildlife Refuge, 57

D

Dakota Sioux, 80
Daniels, Paul, 7, 173
Daylight, 31, 40, 52, 55-56, 70, 73, 82-84, 89, 101, 126, 147, 172, 188
Decoying, 96
"Deercoying", 125
Deer & Deer Hunting Magazine, 8, 161, 165, 172
Deer management, 5, 129-134, 136-137, 140-141, 167-169, 173, 187
Digital, 121-123
Dominance, 25-26, 32, 35
Dominant, 13, 16, 25, 31, 36, 40-46
Dougherty, Craig, 7, 173, 176
Drives, 6, 31, 69, 107
Drop tines, 114-115
Durkin, Pat, 3, 7, 174

E

Elevation, 62, 102
Estrus, 25, 35-37, 39-40, 53, 82, 92, 95, 106
Eyesight, 16

F

"f" setting, 123
Fawn bleat, 94
Feeding, 7, 22, 24, 26, 36, 50, 56-57, 63-65, 76-77, 81, 89-92, 102, 105-106, 125, 146-147, 152, 188
Fence, 12-13, 15, 46, 61, 65, 150
Fertilizer, 144, 150, 157
Fighting, 15-16, 25-26, 29, 31-32, 36, 40, 55, 87, 93-94, 107, 150
Film, 40, 81, 119, 121-126
Finger Lakes, 161, 182
Flehmening, 34, 37
Florida, 8, 86
Focus, 6, 121, 124, 126, 163, 165
Food plot, 24, 65, 77, 139-140, 142, 146, 149-151, 155-158, 188-189
Food, 5, 22, 24-25, 50, 55-57, 63-65, 71-72, 75, 77, 84, 101-102, 104, 106, 110, 133, 139-140, 142-144, 146-147, 149-152, 154-158, 169, 178, 188-189
Forage, 146-147, 150-152, 155-157
Frost-seeding, 156
Fuji velvia, 122
Full moon, 57, 80-87, 89, 96, 106
Funnels, 35, 63-64

G

Genetics, 86, 111, 114, 116
Georgia, 16, 86
Gitzo, 123
Grunts, 19-21, 34, 76, 93-94

H

Haingray, Don, 173
Hamilton, Joe, 169
Hardwoods, 140, 188
Harness, 67
Hearing, 15-16
Herd, 31, 34-35, 39, 87, 96, 99, 111-112, 132, 134, 136, 145
Hero shot, 126
Hofacker, Al, 3, 7, 174
Home range, 57
Hormones, 34, 50, 55, 57
Humidity, 50, 63

I

Inside spread, 115-116, 133

J

Jambers, George, 173
Joseph, Joseph, Dr., 175
Jump, 11-12, 41, 65, 131, 134, 163

K

Kickers, 114

L

Lambase, 100
Language, 26, 34, 93
Laroche, Wayne, 80, 86, 99
Latitude, 52, 80-81, 83, 86
Lenses, 6, 121, 123, 126
Licking branch, 32, 34, 44, 64, 76, 90-92
Light meter, 122
Lingle, Ben 173
Lip-curl, 34, 83

M

Maine, 80, 84-85, 110
Management, 5, 111, 113, 129-134, 136-137, 139-142, 144, 151, 156, 158, 167-169, 173, 187
Mast, 57, 71-73, 75, 102, 142, 145
Mock scrape, 65, 158
Moon, 35, 50, 57, 80-87, 89-90, 92-96, 99-100, 106, 172
Mowing, 152, 156-158

N

National Weather Service, 67
Nightfall, 46, 57, 105, 172
Nikon, 121
Nocturnal, 55, 71, 101-102, 105, 135
Nutrition, 86-87, 106, 111, 113, 139, 146, 149, 151-152, 155, 157

O

O'Connor, Jack, 163
Oathout, Dave, 173-174

P

Pallets, 126
Pavlov, 178
Pecking order, 31-32, 34, 43
Personality, 25
pH, 113, 149-152, 155, 157
Photography, 1, 6, 8, 16, 29, 36, 120-126, 165, 177, 179
Photoperiodism, 31
Pope and Young, 65
Post-rut, 5, 31-32, 36, 99-107
Predators, 24, 50, 61, 85, 178

Primary scrapes, 76, 91
Property layout, 133, 140
Provia, 122

Q

Quality Deer Management, 5, 129-134, 136-137, 140, 167, 169, 173

R

Random scrapes, 91
Ratios, 35-36, 50, 55-56, 84, 86, 134
Rattling, 76-77, 92, 94-96, 107, 178
Recovery time, 36
Research facility, 8, 15, 61, 83, 131, 144, 146, 151, 167
Rice, Terry, 7, 173
Ridge, 62-64, 91
Rub lines, 8, 35, 92
Rubbing, 29, 31-36, 40, 44, 55, 64, 87, 92, 104, 134
Rubs, 19, 33, 63, 76, 84-85, 92-93, 104
Rue Enterprises, 123-124
Rue, Lenny 165
Rue, Leonard Lee III, 16
Rut, 5, 12, 15, 24-27, 29, 31-36, 39, 46, 53-57, 61, 63-64, 69-72, 76-77, 79-87, 89-91, 93-96, 99-102, 104-107, 134
Rutting moon, 35, 57, 80, 82-83, 86-87, 89-90, 92-96, 99

S

Sanctuary, 140-142, 144, 147, 158, 183
Scent, 25, 32-35, 61, 63, 67, 75, 92, 97
ScentLok, 75
Schmidt, Dan, 3, 7, 174
Scouting, 70-71, 90, 165, 169, 172, 183
Scrapes, 19, 32, 34, 63, 65, 73, 76, 85, 90-92, 94
Scraping, 29, 31-36, 40, 52, 55-56, 64, 87, 90, 92, 102, 134
Security, 146-147
Seeking phase, 34-35, 39, 87, 96
Self-timer, 126
Setups, 125, 142
Sex ratio, 87, 96, 136
Sex urge, 101
Sexual advances, 40
Shutter, 123-126
Signpost, 72, 92
Smell, sense of, 15, 54, 60-61
Smoky Mountain National Park, 125
Snorts, 34, 42-43, 93, 95
Snort-wheeze, 20, 42
Soil, 109, 139, 149-152, 155-158, 177
South Carolina, 86
Sparring, 26-27, 34, 36, 76-77, 107
Spraying, 97, 152, 157-158
Stages, 151, 161-162, 167, 169
Stands, 8, 12, 36, 67, 71, 82, 105, 177, 179, 183

Stickers, 114-115
Strategy, 63, 65, 71, 75, 77, 89, 91, 97, 100-101, 105-107, 134
Stress, 36, 110, 113, 134, 157
Stump Sitters, 165
Subordinate, 13, 36, 40-46
Suppressers, 46, 49

T

Taxidermy, 126
TDM, 129, 131, 169
Telemetry, 101
Telephoto, 121, 123, 165
Temperature, 35, 50, 52, 54, 83-84, 155-156, 188
Tending grunt, 94-95
Tennessee, 86
Territory, 24-25, 34, 73, 87, 90-91
Testosterone, 23, 25-26, 30-32, 34, 36, 52, 54-55, 86, 111
Texas, 8, 86, 96, 113, 140, 168, 173, 178
Thanksgiving, 84, 106
Thermals, 62
Thomas, Keith, 50
Topo map, 67, 102
Tracks, 76-77, 105
Traditional Deer Management, 129
Trailing grunt, 94
Trails, 64-66, 72-73, 81, 90-91, 189
Trails, 64-66, 72-73, 81, 90-91, 189
Transition zones, 64, 90
Treestands, 73, 75
Triggers, 5, 29, 46, 49, 82
Tripod, 6, 121-123, 126
Twain, Mark ,124

U

University of Georgia, 16
Urine, 35, 45, 53, 92

V

Velvet, 24, 26, 29-32, 34, 70
Velvet-peeling, 55
Vermont, 80
Vocalization, 25-26, 40, 43, 93-94

W

Weather, 50, 52, 57, 67, 76-77, 83, 86, 96, 113, 150
Wheeze, 42, 46, 93-95
Wind, 15, 53-54, 61-65, 67, 75, 97, 100, 102, 131, 142

Y

Yearling, 35, 76-77, 85-86, 94, 96, 101, 109-110, 112-113, 131, 133, 188

Z

Zoom lens, 122-123